REAL
FOOD

ALSO BY MARIAN TRACY

Cooking Fondue

The Mushroom Cookbook

The New Casserole Cookery

The Art of Making Real Soups

The Shellfish Cookbook

200 Main Course Dishes

Parties from the Freezer

The Picnic Book – 100 Outdoor Meals

Casserole Cookery Complete
(combined edition, revised and enlarged)

The Peasant Cookbook

Complete Chicken Cookery

Coast-to-Coast Cookery (editor)

East-West Book of Rice Cookery

More Casserole Cookery

Cooking under Pressure

The Care and Feeding of Friends

Casserole Cookery (with Nino Tracy)

Marian Tracy

REAL FOOD

*Simple,
Sensuous &
Splendid*

The Viking Press New York

First published in 1978 by The Viking Press
625 Madison Avenue, New York, N.Y. 10022

Published simultaneously in Canada by
Penguin Books Canada Limited

Some of the reflections and ponderings in a few of
the chapter essays—"A Pleasure of Fungi," "A Lift of Picnics,"
"A Discrimination of Rice and Pasta," "A Liveliness of Shellfish,"
"A Nourishment of Soups and Stews"—have appeared in a somewhat
different form in the introduction to the following books
of mine, as have some of the recipes:
THE MUSHROOM COOKBOOK—Doubleday and Company, Inc., 1968
THE PICNIC BOOK—100 OUTDOOR MEALS—Charles Scribner's Sons, 1957
THE EAST-WEST BOOK OF RICE COOKERY—The Viking Press, 1952
paperback—Dover Publications, Inc., 1977
THE SHELLFISH COOKBOOK—The Bobbs-Merrill Company, Inc., 1965
THE ART OF MAKING REAL SOUPS—Doubleday and Company, Inc., 1967

LIBRARY OF CONGRESS CATALOGING IN PUBLICATION DATA
Tracy, Marian Coward.
Real food.
Includes index.
1. Cookery. I. Title.
TX715.T759   641.5   77-21569
ISBN 0-670-59030-4

Printed in the United States of America
Set in Linotype Electra

For Ellen Rogers Coward

"The book of Cookery has out grown the Bible, and I fear is read oftener; to be sure, it is more in use. . . ."

—William Penn, *Fruits of an Active Life*

"Of all the books produced since the most re-mote ages by human talents and industry those only that treat of cooking are, from a moral point of view, above suspicion."

—Joseph Conrad, in a preface to *A Handbook of Cookery for a Small House* by Jessie Conrad

Contents

Introduction

For me, food has been a continuing adventure, and it still is. I don't remember when my enthrallment with the sight, scent, color, taste, and texture of food began, but it was long ago when I was very young. We ate extremely well at home, which I took for granted, assuming that everyone did the same. But even then I was fascinated by references to food or dishes that I had not yet seen or tasted, and I still am.

First it was the toasted cheese and black bread in *Heidi* by Johanna Spyri (very good) and then the fresh milk warm from the cow in Louisa May Alcott's *Eight Cousins* (absolutely revolting). Somewhat later I puzzled at the strange food called yogurt that was spooned up from time to time in Thomas Mann's *Magic Mountain*. But now that yogurt has become part of everyday life in this country, I reread the book without even noticing its presence. I was fascinated with the fruit durian when I first read about it in *The World Was My Garden* by David Fairchild, because it was said to have an ambrosial flavor when ripe, rotten, and stinking. I am less eager to taste it now. Lemon grass, which has the flavor of lemon but the look and texture of a scallion, I first encountered in Rosemary Brissenden's *South East Asian Cooking*; it sounded so tempting but I could find it only in dried form.

While I was growing up and being lured by the unfamiliar, I was eating food of a quality that is mostly unattainable now, even though I have available to me within a few city blocks nearly every known food from all over the civilized world—everything, that is, except an edible, ripe tomato.

When my family first went to live in the Washington, D.C., area, there was a housing shortage. In desperation and with what must have been serious misgivings, my parents rented a house in Virginia, a very pleasant place on a couple of acres with the most inspired planting for good food that I have ever known, along with some chicken houses, fenced-in yards, and chickens. I don't know how one rents chickens (probably we bought them), nor do I remember what happened to them when we moved away more than five years later.

The permanent planting I remember very clearly. There were many more apple trees than we could possibly use—perhaps thirty-five or forty—producing red apples for eating out of hand and Grimes Goldens for pies and applesauce. There were two sour cherry trees, again for pies, a damson plum tree, a Seckel pear, a native persimmon tree with small yellow fruits that were not ripe and edible until after the first frost, two nondescript peach trees, a Bartlett pear tree that had only one pear in the time we were there, and a long, lovely grape arbor with Concord grapes. I remember asparagus plants, strawberry beds, raspberry bushes, and, outside the garden enclosure, perhaps a dozen red currant bushes with fruits like tiny droplets of blown glass. The ducks that we added to the flock of chickens used to like these currants when they escaped from the chicken yards, as they did from time to time. I am less clear about the annual planting, although I know there were tomatoes, peas, corn, leaf lettuce, potatoes, scallions, and radishes.

In those days we had a wonderful woman from Lancaster, Pennsylvania, who did our cooking with extraordinary skill. She stayed with us even during later years when we had moved away from that uncommon garden. I did almost no cooking myself until just before I left home for my first apartment.

New and unfamiliar foods often came to me through the men in my life, those who were close in different ways at different times. Not unnaturally, the first was my father, who showed me my first "foreign food" shop, a German bakery where we bought pfeffernüsse and springerle for Christmas. My bachelor uncle once sent me at college a very large box of food from a Sicilian confectioner, quite unlike anything that other families sent my friends. There was an enormous cake made of hazelnuts and reeking of rum (a special treat in a women's college in those days), a man-sized shoebox full of pistachio nuts, and a dress box filled with macaroons. One man took me to the old Central Market in Washington, when it was still good, and gave me my first memorable taste of unsalted butter. Another sent me a Stilton cheese in port wine that delighted me far more than a bottle of perfume would have; I remember that he once ordered mushrooms under glass for me at dinner—very impressive, since the boys I grew up with were still taking me to drive-ins for hamburgers. Then another man, Nino Tracy, who had learned to cook in Hawaii and New York, brought a provocative ethnic mix of people and food into my life. He cooked and we talked, got married, grew some herbs, searched for varied seasonings (often scarce at that time), worked our separate ways, and, together, wrote a cookbook, *Casserole Cookery*.

Later, suddenly alone, I came to New York with its dazzling variety of foods, spices, and people from many countries, and the adventure quickened. I went on to write more about food, in a regular newspaper column, in magazine articles, and in books, always looking for new ways with food. Once I broke away from the city for a decade, but I missed the excitement and the variety, and I returned, older and quieter but still loving it.

This book is a distillation of the books I have written, the things I have learned about food and cooking, and the things I am still learning. Some of the recipes are taken from those other books, but many more are new.

Cooking and eating are more fun these days, as large numbers of people are finding out. Stoves are more manageable and more easily cleaned than they were in the days of the coal stoves, heart- and room-warming though they were. (I was reminded of those days recently when checking something in Jessie Conrad's A *Handbook of Cookery for a Small House* and finding myself sidetracked by instructions on how one must build a fire an hour and a half before cooking.) I am delighted to have a good gas stove, a refrigerator with a freezing unit, and multiple choices for menu planning, thanks to the good markets in my neighborhood. Seasonal food always tastes best, of course, but it isn't always convenient or accessible.

There are three or four houses in the apple orchard where we once lived (not surprising when you think that there are twice as many people in the world than there were in 1930), and life is not the same, but I would not want the old days back. Once it was a status symbol to have someone to do your cooking, but now it is a status symbol and a joy to do your own. I still don't like to clean, but I like to cook and to have whatever I want at whatever time I want it. There is a fascinating variety of foods available everywhere now, which seems a miracle to those of us with long memories, and there are hundreds of cookbooks on all kinds of cooking, some very bad but enough good ones to lift the spirit and to satisfy the most eager culinary adventurer.

Growing up in a family of healthy, light eaters, I am amused but relieved to find that people are discovering belatedly the blessings of a menu made up of a few carefully chosen and prepared dishes rather than a nondescript profusion. Now, it is easy to concentrate on the quality of the dishes and the logistics and economy of serving them. A well-designed menu is a work of art, requiring skills not unlike those of a good juggler. One must consider the weather and the occasion as well as the amount of time one has for cooking and eating and the state of one's personal economy, but by far the most important consideration is what will give the most pleasure to those who will eat the meal. With experience, you do this unconsciously. The best menu, in my view, is a brief one with dishes that vary and complement one another in flavor, color, texture, and in the manner of presentation.

In such a book as this, which covers so much of my life, it would not be possible to thank all the people who have given me stimulus, knowledge, and support, but these stand out: Sally Adams, Caleb Bevans, Ed Delafield, Jean Evans, Karin and Svend Fennow, Mary and Kent Hamaker, Laulette Hanson, Jean Lapolla, and Bill Moore and his parents (known to an astonishing number of people as Aunt Jo and Unkie). I am particularly grateful to my brother Horace Coward for his tactful encouragement and prodding over a long period of years. Without him, and my editor, Barbara Burn, this book might not have been completed.

REAL
FOOD

An Enticement of Appetizers

John D. MacDonald says in one of his mysteries: "Some of the small sybaritic enhancements of life are worth far more than they cost." This seems to be especially true of many delightful concoctions we traditionally serve as accompaniments to preprandial drinks.

For a simple cold appetizer that is also a tactful gesture for those who worry about calories and cholesterol, serve crudités, melon balls in wine, fresh pineapple with curry, or marinated mushrooms. Some recipes in this chapter can be made ahead and kept on hand in jars for guests who drop in unexpectedly. Simple hot hors d'oeuvre include Saratoga chips, French-fried eggplant fingers, and benne (or sesame) seed cocktail wafers. These may be prepared in advance and heated at the last minute.

For a more important cold hors d'oeuvre, you could serve pimiento cheese or chicken-liver pâté with good French bread, media dolma, or kumquats with cream cheese. Hot hors d'oeuvre, too, can run the international gamut: gougère, tiropetes, pissaladière, or whitebait. These take more time to prepare but for a special occasion can be as impressive as they are delicious.

Whatever you choose to make and serve, keep the hors d'oeuvre tray simple and uncluttered, but strive for interesting combinations of texture, taste, and color. Indiscriminate profusion is never very alluring, and too much food will miss the point, by satisfying rather than stimulating the appetite. Use some attractive pottery bowls, wooden plates or trays, or small baskets as serving dishes.

It is impossible to judge how many people any dish of appetizers will serve. Just how wildly variable preprandial thirsts and appetites can be I found out when I was living in Annapolis. Friends of mine, the Jalberts, a retired naval couple, decided to have a series of four small cocktail parties rather than one overlarge one, and they had on hand the same amount of food and liquor for each party. The guests at the first party drank very little but ate enthusiastically. The second group drank a little more and ate a little less, while the third group drank still more and ate still less. With the fourth party, the Jalberts had to have more liquor brought in, and the food was barely touched.

✌§ FRESH PINEAPPLE CUBES WITH CURRY

On a hot evening, when it was too hot to cook or eat, an imaginative host served me this dish as an appetizer along with freshly salted nuts. It was perfect with the long drinks that preceded the vitello tonnato,* which had been made with turkey breasts instead of veal—another inspired idea.

1 fresh pineapple
3 tablespoons fresh lime juice
1 teaspoon curry powder
2 tablespoons brandy

Cut the top neatly off the pineapple and set it aside. Slice around the inside of the pineapple, leaving a shell about ½-inch thick. Cut the pineapple into manageable bite-size cubes and discard the central woody core, reserving the excess juice. Blend the pineapple juice with the lime juice, curry, and brandy. Check the seasoning, adding more curry or lime juice to taste. Put the cubes into the pineapple shell and pour the seasoned juice over them. Let stand in the refrigerator for at least 2 hours, more if possible. Serve the pineapple with its leaf-tufted cap jauntily placed on top.

* See index for starred items.

❧ PIERRE'S MELON BALLS IN WHITE WINE

Catering at an army installation during World War II, Pierre Ferro once served cantaloupe melon balls in port wine as an appetizer. The weather was very hot and melon balls were gratefully received, for they were fresh tasting and not too filling. Pierre served them in a glass bowl with toothpicks for spearing. I prefer the more subtle flavor and color of honeydew melon balls in a chilled white wine, although I have sometimes added balls carved from Persian melons.

With a melon baller, scoop balls out of the delicate melon flesh and pile them in a glass bowl with Muscadet, Vouvray, or one of the good domestic white wines. Allow about one bottle for one large honeydew and use your prettiest clear glass bowl to serve them in. I always use some fragile-looking carved wooden picks from Panama.

❧ CHERRY TOMATOES STUFFED WITH GREMOLATA

When I first heard of stuffing cherry tomatoes, I thought it was the height of idiocy, partly because they are so perfect in themselves. But now I have accepted the fact that with a spoonful of something simple they have a special appeal.

1 pint cherry tomatoes
1½ tablespoons finely minced parsley
2 plump cloves garlic, finely minced
1 tablespoon grated lemon rind
olive oil

Cut about ¼-inch off the top of the tomatoes. Turn upside down to let the seeds and liquid drain out. Mix the parsley, garlic, and lemon rind together with your fingers. Put a pinch or two of the mixture in each of the drained tomatoes. Pour a drop or two of olive oil on top, but no more or it gets messy to eat. These may be done ahead and chilled, but I like them at room temperature.

ঙ KUMQUATS AND CREAM CHEESE

A decorative and delectable combination that can be concocted almost instantly if the ingredients are to hand. The cream cheese may be flavored with Roquefort cheese if you like.

1 jar preserved kumquats, drained
1 8-oz. package cream cheese at room temperature
2 tablespoons milk, approximately

Cut the kumquats in half and pull out their inside structure, which comes out very neatly. Thin the softened cheese slightly with the milk. Fill the kumquat halves with the cheese and smooth the tops so they are even with the sides of the kumquat shells. These may be done ahead and chilled or frozen until needed.

ঙ LARGE MUSHROOM CAPS WITH RED CAVIAR

These are beautiful to look at, simple to make, and delicious to eat.

1 lb. large, fresh mushroom caps (save the stems for duxelles*)
juice of ½ lemon
red salmon or lumpfish caviar (1 4-oz. jar)
sour cream (optional)

Parboil the mushroom caps in boiling water with the lemon juice for 2 or 3 minutes. Drain on paper towels. Put a spoonful of the red caviar on each mushroom cap, not more than a half hour before serving. If you like, top with a dollop of sour cream.

✒ GRAVLAX

One of the great and beautiful dishes of the world. My Danish friends first made this for me in a Greenwich Village apartment rather a long time ago, and not much later I had it at their apartment in Copenhagen. Wherever you make it, however, you must have very, very fresh salmon. It is an impressive dish that might star at a special gathering for pre-dinner sipping. When serving it with drinks, arrange it on a platter with a small bowl of mustard, some plates and forks, and perhaps some thin toast with small bowls of freshly salted almonds and marinated mushrooms. If served as a main dish, a mushroom risotto* and cucumber salad are felicitous accompaniments. Follow with sections of honeydew melon, blueberries and strawberries, and coffee, which for me is always espresso.

3–3½ lbs. fresh salmon (center cut or darne),
cleaned, boned and split in half
1 large bunch fresh dill, washed and dried
1 cup coarse salt, kosher or sea
¼ cup sugar
2 tablespoons white or black peppercorns, crushed

Place one half the salmon, skin side down, on a piece of heavy-duty aluminum foil large enough to cover both pieces and set it inside a china or enameled baking dish. Lay the bunch of dill on the salmon. Mix the salt, sugar, and crushed peppercorns well and strew evenly over the dill and the salmon. Place the other half of the fish on top, skin side up. Fold the pieces of aluminum foil together in what used to be called a drugstore wrap before they began to use bags—in other words, a double fold on top and on the ends. Place full heavy cans of food or weights on top and refrigerate for at least 48 hours.

Turn the package over every morning and night so that the marinade seeps through the fish. Each time you turn the package, open it and spoon some juice between the halves; then put them together again and refold the package. When the curing is finished, remove the fish from the marinade. Scrape off the dill and the seasonings and pat dry with paper towels. Wrap the halves in fresh pieces of foil, and store in the refrigerator until wanted. To serve, place each half on a chopping block and slice thin on the slant as one does with smoked salmon. Serve with mustard and dill sauce. If it is served as a main course, add toast and cucumber salad to the platter.

MUSTARD AND DILL SAUCE (SWEDISH)

4 tablespoons dark, highly seasoned prepared mustard
1 teaspoon dry mustard
3 tablespoons sugar
2 tablespoons white vinegar
⅓ cup vegetable oil
3 tablespoons fresh chopped dill

In a small, deep bowl, mix the two mustards, sugar, and vinegar to a paste. With a wire whisk slowly beat in the oil until it forms a thick mayonnaise-like emulsion. Stir in the chopped dill. The sauce may be kept refrigerated in a lightly covered jar for several days but will probably need to be shaken vigorously or beaten with a whisk to mix the ingredients before serving. Makes ¾ cup.

⋙ CRUDITÉS

At one time uninspired and uncaring hostesses were wont to serve carrot sticks and celery sticks as hors d'oeuvre, with some commercially prepared nuts if you were lucky. Nowadays people are more interested in eating and preparing food, and many more interesting and varied raw vegetables are excitingly presented with the pre-dinner drinks. As crudités, these have been well known and beautifully served in France for years, but they are especially appropriate in this country now that people are more concerned about keeping their weight down. Some people serve dips with these vegetables to slow down the effect of alcoholic intake, but I often choose not to. I'd rather give drinkers some cheese or nuts and serve the raw vegetables unadorned with the exception of coarse salt, preferably sea salt. Any of the following vegetables separately or together will be both an appetizing and attractive prelude to dinner.

raw asparagus, trimmed
raw kohlrabi, peeled and cut in julienne fashion
raw fennel (the anise-flavored bulb), cut in thin strips
very young raw broad beans (which is to say, limas)
fresh raw peas
cauliflower flowerets

⌦ BAGNA CAUDA

A simple, savory, and aromatic dip, this is served hot in Italy as a snack with cold raw vegetables (hence the name, which means warm bath), and glasses of local red wine. In the United States pace-setting hostesses serve bagna cauda in fondue pots with platters of cold, crisp raw vegetables and cocktails. It is best not to have more than six or eight guests hovering around one pot.

½ cup (1 stick) unsalted butter
½ cup olive oil
6 cloves garlic, peeled and sliced
1 2-oz. can anchovies in oil, chopped
ice-cold raw vegetables (endive, cucumber strips, carrots,
green and red pepper rings, broccoli or cauliflower flowerets,
white radishes, and so on)

In a fondue pot or heavy saucepan heat the butter and oil for a few minutes without letting the mixture come to a boil. Add garlic and anchovies and stir. Serve in a fondue pot over low heat or in a pan on a warming tray. Dry off the ice-cold vegetables and cut them into neat and manageable strips or pieces. Encourage your guests to dip an end of each piece in the mixture. Serves 8 to 10.

Serve before broiled steak; watercress; Paris-Brest*.

❧ CARPACCIO

Among the many dishes of the world that I have known, mused upon, and eaten from time to time, there was never any question when Nino's son and I ate together as to what we would choose, at home or in a restaurant. It was always some form of raw beef, whether steak tartare with its trimmings or simply one-inch cubes of prime steak, salted and peppered lightly, with nothing else added. More and more timid people who once used to panic at the sight of uncooked beef are nowadays happily eating carpaccio, a variation on the steak-tartare theme, served in very thin slices with several different sauces. Joseph Wechsberg, writing in *Gourmet* magazine, reports that the owner of Harry's Bar in Venice claims to have named carpaccio after one of his favorite Renaissance artists and serves it with a very lemony mayonnaise. Many of the sauces traditionally served with beef fondue are equally good for carpaccio. I like an oil sauce made with walnuts and garlic (see capellini*) as well as apricot and horseradish sauce*. Carpaccio is most often served as an appetizer, but I like it as a main dish, especially in the summer.

1½ lb. sirloin tip or London broil (very finest quality)
lemon mayonnaise (see below)

It is best to slice the meat yourself with a very sharp knife, which can be easily accomplished if the meat is put in the freezing unit just long enough to firm it up before slicing. Most restaurants serve it sliced paper thin, but I prefer it cut to the thickness of cardboard. The slices look very handsome arranged on a dull black platter or a dish of some other plain color that will harmonize with the beef. If carpaccio is to be served with drinks, cut the slices in halves or thirds and provide toothpicks for dipping in the sauce or sauces. Serves 6 as appetizer.

LEMON MAYONNAISE (BLENDER VERSION)

1 egg
2 tablespoons fresh lemon juice
2 teaspoons grated lemon rind
salt, white pepper
1 cup oil (not olive)

Put the egg, lemon juice, lemon rind, salt, white pepper, and ¼ cup of the oil in the container of the blender. Blend well. With the motor still running pour the rest of the oil in slowly until it is well mixed. Remove and serve with the carpaccio (or with cucumber sticks), or chill until needed. Makes 1 cup.

❧ CHILE VERDE CON QUESO

Even a few months in Santa Fe, New Mexico, can leave one with an intense longing to go back and an equally intense longing—but more realistic and easier to satisfy—for the very subtle sharpness of green chilies combined in almost any way with cheese. After hearing my friends there describe how even their accustomed hands got blistered when handling fresh green chilies, I prefer to use the canned variety. This dish is what Irma Rombauer called an icebreaker, when it is served in the living room with before-dinner drinks. It certainly does get everyone milling around in a companionable way. The traditional accompaniment is Fritos or tostadas, but French bread is just as good.

1 large onion, chopped
2 tablespoons butter
1 1-lb. can tomatoes, drained and diced
1 4-oz. can green chilies, drained and chopped
½ lb. Monterey Jack or mild longhorn cheese, diced
½ teaspoon marjoram
½ teaspoon salt
Fritos, tostadas, or French bread

Sauté the onion in butter in a skillet. Add the diced and drained tomatoes, green chilies, cheese, marjoram, and salt. Cook over low heat until the cheese is melted. Transfer to an earthenware fondue pot and put over low heat. Give each person a small plate of Fritos or tostadas or pieces of French bread with crust on it. If using bread, give your guests forks. Serves 4 to 6.

Serve before sliced roast beef; beet and endive salad (without the walnuts)*; orange sherbet with grated unsweetened chocolate.

⋞§ MEDIA DOLMA

The Greeks stuff all sorts of edibles—squash, peppers, eggplants, melons, grape leaves, and so on. One of my favorite appetizers is this traditional Greek way of serving stuffed mussels.

½ cup raw rice
¼ cup olive oil
1 chopped medium onion
1 teaspoon allspice
salt, pepper
¼ cup pine nuts or pignolias
2 tablespoons dried currants
2 dozen mussels

Cook the rice in oil with the chopped onion until golden. Add a cup of water, the allspice, salt, pepper, pine nuts, and currants. Bring to a boil, cover, lower the heat, and simmer for 15 or 20 minutes or until the rice is tender and the liquid is absorbed. Meanwhile, scrub the mussels very carefully until the shells are smooth and gleaming. Put in an inch of water, bring to a boil, and simmer until the shells open. Remove and drain, reserving the liquid. Remove the top shell from each mussel and discard. Fill the mussels with the rice stuffing, pressing down. Place the filled shells in a shallow casserole with the reserved liquid in which the mussels were cooked.

Cover and bake in 325° oven for 45 minutes or cook them, covered, over low heat on top of stove until water evaporates. Serves 4.

Serve as a first course before lamb and okra stew*; dandelion salad with sliced hard-cooked eggs; pideh*; pear and custard pie.

⇜ BENNE SEED COCKTAIL WAFERS

In Charleston, South Carolina, home-grown sesame seeds are called benne, for some reason. To toast them, put the seeds on a dry skillet over medium heat and cook until they jump in the pan. Stir them around until all are lightly brown. These toasted seeds can be stored in a glass jar indefinitely.

½ cup toasted benne or sesame seeds
2 cups sifted flour
½ teaspoon salt
½ cup shortening (butter or margarine)

Mix the benne seeds with the salt and flour. With a pastry blender or two knives, cut the shortening into the flour until it is coarsely mixed. Add a small amount of ice water, a few drops at a time, and mix lightly with a fork until you have a stiff dough. Roll the dough as thin as cardboard on a lightly floured board. Cut into thin strips measuring 1 inch by 2 inches, or use a small biscuit cutter. Arrange the strips on a buttered cookie sheet and bake in a preheated 350° oven for 10 to 12 minutes. Makes 40 or more depending upon size.

⇜ SARATOGA CHIPS

Potato chips have been so mistreated commercially that the home-made and original version seems a startling new and entrancing dish.

Basically this recipe involves one simple ingredient treated with knowledge and respect. The story goes that a chef at a hotel in Saratoga, home of the famous racetrack, became so annoyed by an over-finicky and bossy customer that he made the slices of potato paper thin and thus began a popular new fashion. Nevertheless, the fashion is said to have been well known long before that on the European continent.

Peel a few large baking potatoes and slice them paper thin. Soak the slices in ice water for about 2 hours and pat dry with paper towels. Fry a few at a time in about 2 inches of vegetable oil heated to 375° until they are crisp and golden. Remove and drain on paper towels. Sprinkle with coarse salt, preferably sea salt. Serve immediately or keep warm until serving time.

✑ FRENCH-FRIED EGGPLANT

This is one of my favorite vegetables, which is always eagerly sought after at cocktail parties, although it makes a wonderful side dish at dinner.

1 large eggplant (about 2 lbs.)
beer batter (see strawberry fritters*)
oil for deep frying
sea or kosher salt

Peel the eggplant and cut into finger-size pieces. Dip each piece in the beer batter and fry a few at a time in fat heated to 365° until they are lightly browned.

As a side dish, serve with broiled steak or lamb chops; mixed green salad; Irish coffee.

⋧ WHITEBAIT

Whitebait refers to tiny fish of many different species about the size of the inside loop of a paper clip. Served whole and deep-fried, whitebait are delicacies for rich and poor alike. They add a dramatic flourish to a cocktail party, a fillip to jaded palates.

1 lb. whitebait
flour
salt, pepper
oil for deep frying

Season about a cup of flour with salt and pepper in a small paper bag. Shake a few whitebait at a time in the flour until they are all well covered. Heat the fat in a heavy skillet or an electric deep-fat fryer to 350°. Put a handful of the floured fish in the frying basket and fry until crisp. (If too many are done at a time, they will stick together in an unattractive lump.) Drain on paper towels. Serve hot with a small bowl of cold lemon juice to dip the fish in.

Serve as appetizer along with pâté in aspic; toast fingers; cherry tomatoes.

A Charm of Apricots

Izaak Walton in *The Compleat Angler* quotes a Dr. Boteler as saying of strawberries, "Doubtless God could have made a better berry but doubtless he never did." It has been mistakenly attributed to Francis Bacon and others ever since, but instead of misquoting I choose instead to misapply it—to dried apricots. Since these contain the glorious and concentrated essence of all apricots, they have a more intense flavor than the fresh. The color, too, is often more beautiful in the dried fruit, a montage of all the sunsets I've ever seen. There are exceptions to that rule. Near my apartment is a health-food store where I buy raw shelled nuts, which are much cheaper than inferior ones elsewhere, and good stone-ground flour. I cast an eye from time to time at the strange items that abound there and am occasionally startled to see dark brown dried apricots, not a bad color for some things but rather depressing for apricots.

I like apricots in many, many dishes—meat loaves, soufflés, mousses, ice creams, pilafs. I like them cooked with almonds, in turnovers, breads, chutneys, in a sour-cream and horseradish sauce, and to eat out of hand.

Indians and fur traders used to sustain themselves on long journeys with pemmican, a dried, thinly sliced, lean meat pounded to shreds, mixed with melted fat, some bone marrow, and a few handfuls of dried wild fruit, and packed into rawhide sacks. Pemmican must have made a wonderful, nourishing snack en route. Even in these days of quick trips to the ends of the world, there are less remote places that can be reached only by car or bus, and all you can find at bus stops are dreary fly-specked peanut-butter crackers. Now I carry my own present-day equivalent of pemmican, which is tidy, easily portable, attractive, and satisfying—a plastic bag filled with a combination of

14

dried apricots (not soaked or cooked) and shelled hazelnuts or almonds.

Even when I am not on a trip, I often serve up the same treat for breakfast or for an unscheduled attack of hunger. On a dark plate it makes a handsome still life, much more exciting to look at than a bowl of cereal or peanuts, and even richer in life-giving elements.

⋙ APRICOT CHUTNEY

This was one of my favorite chutneys from the days before mangoes were so plentiful and widely available, and it still is.

1½ cups dried apricots, quartered
1 cup coarsely chopped onions
6 tablespoons granulated sugar
2 cups water
1 cup cider vinegar
½ cup blanched almonds, grated or ground very fine
2 dried hot chili peppers (about two inches long), crumbled or grated
1 tablespoon finely chopped garlic
2 teaspoons ground coriander
1 teaspoon yellow mustard seed
1 tablespoon grated fresh ginger root
1 2-inch cinnamon stick
1 teaspoon salt
juice of ½ lemon

Cook the apricots, onions, sugar, water, and vinegar in a stainless steel or enamel saucepan and stir until the sugar is dissolved. Turn the heat down and simmer for about 10 to 15 minutes or until the apricots are tender and the mixture is thick. Add the rest of the ingredients. Check the seasonings, adding more according to taste. Store the chutney in the refrigerator but serve at room temperature. (It does not keep more than 2 or 3 weeks.) Makes 2 cups.

Serve with broiled chicken breasts; sautéed mushrooms and kasha*; tossed green salad; Paris-Brest*.

✑ CRANBERRIES IN APRICOT BRANDY

This is a beautiful and simple accompaniment to a turkey, and in a beautiful jar it makes a pretty gift.

1 lb. cranberries
1 cup apricot brandy, domestic
2 cups sugar
1 cup slivered almonds (optional)

Pick over the cranberries and discard any imperfect ones. Rinse and shake dry. Put the cranberries, apricot brandy, and sugar in a pan with water to cover and boil for about 12 to 14 minutes. Do not drain. Add the almonds if you like. Pour into a jar or serving bowl and keep in the refrigerator until needed. Makes 2 to 3 cups.

✑ APRICOT AND HORSERADISH SAUCE

1 cup dried, diced apricots, soaked 1 or 2 hours in water
2–3 tablespoons freshly grated horseradish
or 1½ bottles horseradish, drained
1 cup sour cream

Drain the apricots and combine with the other ingredients in a blender. Blend together and chill. Makes 2 cups of sauce.

Serve with cold tongue or ham; whole green beans; potato pancakes*.

✑ APRICOTS AND COGNAC

Alice B. Toklas always kept prunes in port wine on hand for a suitable occasion. I like the sight and scent and flavor of dried apricots, and if possible I try to have dried apricots soaking in cognac in the cupboard just in case. Apricots should stand for at least 24 hours in the cognac but can get mushy if kept too long.

1 lb. dried apricots
½ cup granulated sugar
cognac or armagnac to cover

Combine the ingredients and chill in the refrigerator. When serving, place some of the liquor along with the apricots in each dish. If you are feeling reckless about calories, sprinkle the fruit with slivered almonds and top with lightly whipped cream. Serves 6.

Serve after chicken livers in wine sauce with wild rice; Bibb lettuce with oil-and-lemon-juice dressing.

❧ COLD PORK TENDERLOIN
WITH ROSEMARY-SCENTED APRICOT ASPIC

Pork tenderloin is the long piece of meat cut from a pork-loin roast. Some butchers will bone the roast specially, but you can do so easily yourself by cutting the main section (the pork-chop part) away from the bone. This cut is comparable to beef tenderloin, although of course it is much smaller. You can also substitute Canadian bacon if you can get a single piece weighing about 2 to 3 pounds.

2 pork tenderloins or 1 piece Canadian bacon (see above)
flour, salt, pepper
1 sprig fresh rosemary or ¾ teaspoon dried rosemary
3 tablespoons fresh lemon juice
1½ envelopes unflavored gelatin
2 cups apricot juice
pinch of salt

Dust the tenderloins with the seasoned flour. Place on a rack in a preheated 350° oven for 45 to 50 minutes or until meat is tender and cooked through. Remove and let cool. Chill in the refrigerator. Chop the fresh rosemary (or crumble the dried) and soak in lemon juice. Soften the gelatin in ½ cup of the apricot juice. Heat the rest of the juice in a saucepan, add the softened gelatin, and stir over low heat until dissolved. Remove from heat and add salt and the lemon juice and rosemary. Chill the mixture until it starts to thicken (about 1 hour).

Place the chilled pork on a platter but not on the one you plan to use for serving. Brush or spoon the slightly thickened apricot aspic on the meat and return it to the refrigerator and chill until it becomes a firm glaze (about 1 or 2 hours). Remove from the refrigerator and brush or spoon on another layer of aspic. If the aspic has become too thick, warm it slightly until it liquifies. Chill the meat until the second layer of aspic becomes firm and repeat the procedure once more. Pour the leftover aspic into a pie plate and chill. To serve, transfer the glazed pork to a plain dark or glass platter. Dice the thin aspic from the pie plate and spoon around the meat for a professional sparkle.

Serve with Bibb lettuce with cream dressing*; Marlborough apple pie*.

MEAT LOAF WITH APRICOTS

This is for the growing number of people who like meat loaf without tomatoes in any form—fresh or canned, in the meat loaf or over it. It is baked and served in a Mexican loaf pan.

1½ lbs. ground beef
1 egg
⅔ cup dried apricots, cut in quarters
½ cup chopped scallions
⅓ cup chopped fresh parsley
1 teaspoon aromatic dried mint
½ teaspoon cinnamon
salt, pepper

Mix meat and egg with your fingers. Add the rest of ingredients and pat into buttered pottery loaf pan. Bake in preheated 350° oven for 1 hour or more. Serves 4 to 6.

Serve with spoon bread*; orange and black-olive salad*; coffee ice cream, with chocolate syrup.

✌§ LAMB WITH RICE AND APRICOTS

I first read of this dish in Josephine Tey's *Singing Sands,* where it was described in glowing terms by a man who turned out to be the murderer

3 tablespoons butter or other shortening
1½ lbs. lamb shoulder, cut into chunks
salt, pepper
¼ teaspoon cinnamon
¼ teaspoon nutmeg
1 teaspoon grated lemon rind
2 cups chicken broth
⅔ cup dried apricots, quartered
1½ cups rice
1 cup white wine
more salt
¼ cup melted butter

Melt the butter or shortening in a Dutch oven or heavy stew pot. Season the lamb with salt and pepper, cinnamon, nutmeg, and lemon rind. Sauté the meat in the butter until it is well browned on all sides. Add the chicken broth and bring to a boil. Cover the pot and turn the heat down low to simmer until the lamb is almost tender (about 1 hour). Add the apricots, rice, and wine, and more salt if needed. Bring to a boil again, cover, and simmer for about 20 minutes. Remove lid, fluff the rice with a fork, and turn the meat onto a warm, deep pottery platter. Drizzle the melted butter over it and serve hot. Serves 4 to 6.

Serve with Bibb and watercress salad with vinaigrette dressing; lemon-curd tarts*.

ᵉᵇ§ APRICOT SOUFFLÉ

It is rare and wonderful to find apricots or figs in their fresh, fragrant, sun-ripened, almost perfect state, but dried apricots are a constant, concentrated, and compact delight, adding a delicate aroma, flavor, and one of the loveliest of colors to almost any dish. In a soufflé, with the puréed fruit acting as the sauce base, they are, I think, at their blissful best.

½ lb. dried apricots, soaked 1 or 2 hours in water
2 tablespoons sugar
2 egg yolks, slightly beaten
2 tablespoons heavy cream
5 egg whites, beaten stiff

Drain the apricots and purée in electric blender or put them through a food mill. Add sugar, egg yolks, and cream, and stir until thoroughly mixed. Fold in the beaten egg whites gently and put the mixture into a buttered 1-quart casserole or soufflé dish with straight sides. Place the dish on a cookie sheet in a preheated 350° oven. Bake for 25 to 35 minutes (according to the idiosyncrasies of your oven). When done, the soufflé should spring back when *lightly* touched. Serves 4 in small but rich portions.

Serve after ham baked with endive; new potatoes; chilled cucumber sticks; hot biscuits.

⋑ APRICOT MOUSSE

This is a beautiful dessert that can be made ahead and held a day or so in the refrigerator, or even longer in the freezer.

3 cups dried apricot halves, soaked 1 or 2 hours in water
¼ cup granulated sugar
1 teaspoon almond extract
pinch of salt
1 cup heavy cream, whipped

Drain the apricots and mash them into a pulp. Mix the pulp with the sugar, almond extract, and a pinch of salt. Fold in the whipped cream. Spoon the mixture into a covered mold and chill or freeze. To serve the mousse, unmould it onto a platter just before dinner and keep in refrigerator until serving time. Serves 6 to 8.

Serve after veal piccata*, risotto di funghi*, watercress and arugula salad.

An Aroma of Bakings

Despite the superbly cooked food that I took for granted while I was growing up, I remember being very uninterested in the bread we were given. It was not baked at home, and there was not much by way of good bakeries in our small Virginia town at that time. Although I do not remember the bread being as dreadfully squishy as the stuff that passes for bread in the supermarkets now, I didn't like it much. So I usually abstained from eating it except when it was used for my school sandwiches. I didn't like them much either, but no one came up with any alternatives (I can think of many now.)

When I read Johanna Spyri's *Heidi* in those days, I used to be puzzled by an incident that occurred during Heidi's visit to the city, when she was discovered storing white bread in her closet to take home to Peter's grandmother. It was to be a great treat for her in place of her usual black bread, which I always thought sounded much more fascinating. My prejudices became so deeply embedded that I still cannot bring myself to buy, make, or eat even *good* homemade white bread if it has the usual loaf shape. I like long, narrow, crusty French bread, and fat, round Italian bread as full of holes as good Emmenthaler cheese, and I often want a round, flat pideh. Luckily, in New York City, where I have spent half my adult life, I have a varied and fragrant choice.

Nevertheless, I do make bread from time to time as much for the rhythmic pleasure and the wonderful aroma that pervades my apartment as for the taste. I bake when I am not near a good bakery or when I feel the urge to practice one of the most pleasurable and rewarding habits of economy. And I bake because it is one way of controlling the quality and the ingredients of what I eat. (My brother once read me from *Consumer Reports* a shocking story about

22

the bits of unseemly debris that turn up in even the best of mass-produced bread.) French, Italian, Cuban, and Greek breads are just a blend of yeast, good flour, salt, and water. There are no sugar, no fat, and no additives. They don't keep long but they freeze well. The flour does not need to be bread flour, just a good all-purpose brand that has not been subjected to some of the indignities inflicted upon flour such as "refining."

If one bakes often and for a large family, it is worth searching for fresh yeast, which one can buy from a baker. If one bakes only occasionally, as I do, the packaged yeast in the dairy-food case at the supermarket is perfectly adequate so long as it is fresh (it will keep about two weeks in the refrigerator). One does need to use a bit of sugar or honey, though, to get it started. I usually keep the dry, granular yeast on hand because I never know when the yearning to bake might come upon me.

Lacking a sweet tooth, I make very few cakes and only an occasional batch of cookies. The broyage Suisse, however, is a nut meringue that I think is very special and about as far as you can get from the gooey layer cakes of childhood. The meringue is baked in three thin layers with a rich filling between the layers and over the top. I always make a chocolate version because I make it for festive occasions and most of the people I know think it isn't a party unless the dessert is chocolate.

Baking of any kind has never been a matter of routine for me. I enjoy baking of all kinds—gougères, panettones, crumpets, macaroons, oak leaves, benne seed cocktail wafers—and I enjoy it most when I expect some friends or family to come by or am planning a picnic or another sort of feast.

᥍ PIDEH (PITTA, PITA, PETA)

This round, flat bread baked and eaten in many areas around the Mediterranean has many names. The size usually found in the supermarkets these days is about 6 inches in diameter, but I like the 3-inch size, which, according to one bakery, has only 80 calories.

The smaller size appeals to me not only for snacking at home but also as a portable container for the Near Eastern sort of sandwich.

1 envelope active dry yeast
1 tablespoon granulated sugar
¾ cup warm water
1 teaspoon salt
2 cups white all-purpose flour
1 tablespoon olive oil

Put the yeast and sugar in a small bowl and add ½ cup warm water (not much warmer than your hand—if it is too warm the yeast won't rise). Let stand for about 10 minutes, stirring it after 2 or 3 minutes to dissolve the yeast, at which time the mixture should be bubbly and thickened. Dissolve the salt in the remaining ¼ cup of warm water. Put the flour in a large mixing bowl and make a well in the center. Put the yeast mixture and the salted water in the well. Mix with your hands until you get a soft dough. (The amount of flour will vary according to the type of flour and the moisture in the air, so add more or less if it is either gooey or too stiff.) Knead with your hands for 10 to 15 minutes until the dough feels smooth, elastic, and somehow alive (which it is). Add the olive oil and knead some more until it has been absorbed. Cover the bowl loosely with a towel and put it in a draft-free warm place (80°) until it doubles in bulk, about 1 to 2 hours. Then punch it down and knead for about 2 minutes.

Preheat the oven to 400°. Pinch off small pieces of dough not larger than an egg. Roll into balls and then roll or pat them on a lightly floured board until they are about ¼-inch thick. Put them on a lightly oiled cookie sheet and set the pan on the lower rack in the oven and bake for 2 or 3 minutes on each side. The breads should be white and soft. Getting them a light brown in our home ovens would make them too hard. Makes 10 small pidehs.

◆§ PERUVIAN CORN BREAD

This is freely adapted from a recipe my brother's mother-in-law used while living in Peru. Her version was a little heavy for American tastes.

1½ cups cornmeal
½ cup flour
2 eggs
1¼ cups milk
3 tablespoons melted butter
1 cup dried sharp Cheddar cheese
1 cup coarsely chopped onions
salt, pepper

Beat the cornmeal, flour, eggs, and milk together or buzz briefly in the blender. Stir in the melted butter, cheese, onions, salt, and pepper. Pour into a 9 x 9-inch pan that has been lightly buttered. Bake in a preheated 350° oven for 45 to 50 minutes and cut in 3-inch squares while still hot. Serves 4 to 6.

◆§ SPOON BREAD

Spoon bread is, precisely, a soft moist corn bread that is *served* with a spoon. It isn't eaten with the spoon but served on a plate with lots of butter, in place of potatoes or rice and bread. It is simple to make, and there is no such thing as a poor one, though some are richer in eggs than others and some are puffy like a soufflé. White cornmeal, preferably water-ground with flecks of the yellow, is always used, according to the purists—which is to say, all Southerners. On the other hand, the directions will work perfectly well with the yellow cornmeal available in most regions.

1 cup white cornmeal
1 cup boiling water
1 teaspoon salt
1 cup milk
2 or 3 eggs, separated for the fluffy type
2 tablespoons butter or, better yet, bacon drippings

Scald the cornmeal by pouring the boiling water and salt over it in a mixing bowl. Stir in the milk, a little at a time, and the whole eggs if the plain spoon bread is desired. If the fluffy version is wanted, stir in the unbeaten egg yolks and then fold in the whites, which have been beaten stiff. Heat a shallow baking dish with the butter or drippings and turn the spoon bread into the heated fat. Bake in a preheated 350° oven 45 to 50 minutes or until the top is a golden brown. Serve with lots of butter. Serves 4 to 6.

Serve with grilled chicken with chopped onion; pebre salad—a Chilean mishmash of chopped onion, diced tomatoes, hot green chili pepper, olive oil, vinegar, salt, and pepper.

◄§ PISSALADIÈRE

The French provincial answer to pizza and one I greatly prefer, made with a pastry shell that is more delicate than the doughy kind.

1 cup onions, sliced
1 fat clove garlic, minced
¼ cup olive oil
salt, pepper
bay leaf
1 9-inch pie shell, half-baked (about 15 minutes)
⅔ cup black olives, unpitted (the olive-oil-cured kind now available in jars or cans)
1 2-oz. can flat French anchovies

Sauté the onion and garlic in the hot oil and add salt, pepper, and bay leaf. Cook until the onions are a light, even brown and remove the bay leaf. Spread the mixture over the bottom of the pie shell. Rinse the olives, drain well, and strew over the onions, and arrange the anchovies over them. Bake in a preheated 450° to 500° oven for about 15 minutes, or until brown. Serve cut in strips or wedges. If you are serving this as the main meal for some hungry people, double the quantity. This will serve 4 for a light meal.

Serve with lemon chicken*; Armenian pilaf*; sliced orange and cucumber salad with vinaigrette dressing.

⌣ COULIBIAC

In my gastronomic adventuring I have nearly always been delighted by the various concoctions of meats or vegetables or fish or cheese that are baked in coarse or fine doughs throughout the world. The Russians have many versions, such as the small piroshki, which are baked and served with soup, and the larger pirogen, which may have a variety of fillings. Coulibiac, or kulebiaka, has a flaky pastry with a cabbage or a salmon filling. According to people I know who have lived or visited the U.S.S.R., the Russians eat many large meals and use this as *one* of the dishes on the *zakuska* table (like a smorgasbord), but I often serve it as the main dish in a light meal. In this American adaptation I have used a classic (and superb) cream-cheese pastry that is not at all traditional to the Russians, but which goes surprisingly well with the Russian cabbage filling.

CREAM-CHEESE PASTRY

½ cup (1 stick) butter
4 oz. cream cheese
1 cup sifted flour

Cream the butter and cheese until well blended. Add the flour and mix until smooth and no individual ingredient can be seen.

Wrap in aluminum foil or put into a plastic bag and freeze for an hour or so if time is short. Otherwise chill in the refrigerator overnight and remove half an hour before rolling out.

CABBAGE FILLING

1 medium head of green cabbage
1 cup milk
1 cup water
1 tablespoon sugar
¾ cup chopped onions
⅓ cup or ¾ stick butter
½ lb. raw mushrooms, stems and caps chopped
salt, pepper
¾ cup sour cream
1 egg yolk

Quarter the cabbage and remove and discard the hard core. Chop fine. Stew in a deep saucepan in the milk, water, and sugar until limp and well cooked (about 5 minutes). Sauté the onions in the butter until translucent and beginning to color. Add the chopped mushrooms to the pan and fry until the onions become golden. Drain the cabbage well and stir into the onion-mushroom mixture. Add salt and pepper to taste. Stir in the sour cream, blending well. Set aside while, on a lightly floured cloth or board, you roll the pastry less than ¼ inch thick. (It should be thin and crisp after baking.) Arrange the filling on one half the dough and fold the other half over the filling and pinch the sides. Slash the top in a decorative way and paint the top with one egg yolk diluted in 1 tablespoon of water. Slide the coulibiac onto a baking sheet. Bake in a preheated 450° oven for 15 to 20 minutes until well browned and crisp. Serves 6 to 8.

Serve with cucumber and fennel salad; apricot mousse*.

✌ MEAT LOAF BAKED IN A CRUST

A handsome cousin to a meat pot pie, with a much more refined texture, this can be a very decorative dish if some imagination is used in cutting and placing the leftover bits of dough on top.

3 tablespoons butter
⅓ cup finely chopped onions
1½ lbs. ground lean beef
⅓ cup freshly chopped parsley, preferably the flat Italian kind
½ cup milk
⅓ cup freshly ground Parmesan cheese
salt
pie dough for 2 crusts
1 egg plus 2 tablespoons milk

Melt the butter in a skillet and sauté the onions and beef until the onions are translucent and the beef has turned color and released most of its liquid. With a slotted spoon transfer the meat and onions to a bowl. Let cool slightly. Add the parsley, milk, Parmesan cheese, and salt to taste. Divide the pie dough in half and roll each piece into a long rectangle. Trim the sides so that they are straight and save the leftover pieces. Roll or pat the meat mixture onto one dough rectangle so that it is the same shape as the dough, but leave a margin of about 1½ inches on each edge. Place the other piece of dough on top. Crimp the edges together and press down with a fork all around, making a neat design. Cut the leftover pieces into a design and arrange them on the top crust. Beat the egg with the milk, using a wire whisk or a fork, and paint the top with a pastry brush. Bake on a cookie sheet in a preheated 350° oven for about 50 minutes. Serves 4 to 6.

Serve with cucumber salad; creamed mushrooms*; raspberry rice*.

CRANBERRY NUT BREAD

This tangy and colorful loaf is perhaps my favorite of all quick breads. It may be baked in two small bread tins instead of one 9 x 5-inch pan or, for tea, you can make several small round loaves in cans (with one end removed) that once held concentrated orange juice or nuts. It freezes well.

2 cups sifted all-purpose flour
2 teaspoons baking powder
½ teaspoon salt
½ teaspoon baking soda
¼ cup soft butter
1 cup sugar
1 egg
1 teaspoon vanilla
1 cup milk
1½ cups fresh cranberries, ground
1 tablespoon grated orange rind
½ cup chopped walnuts or filberts

Sift the flour, baking powder, salt, and baking soda together. Cream the butter and sugar together until fluffy. Stir in the egg, vanilla, and milk. When thoroughly mixed add the flour mixture, a little at a time, and last of all, the cranberries, orange rind, and nuts. Turn the dough into greased pan or pans. Bake in a preheated 350° oven for 1 hour (a little longer for the regular-size loaf, less for the smaller size), or until the top is firm and springs back at the touch of a finger.

PANETTONE

Of all the yeast doughs made festive with butter, eggs, sweetening, and the candied fruits and nuts traditionally used at holiday time in many countries, I am perhaps fondest of panettone. Nevertheless, they are all delectable—to name a few, English saffron bread, Russian kulich, Danish julekage, and Irish barmbrack, which Lady Gregory used to take to the green room at the Abbey Theatre as a special treat. They all keep well and may be frozen.

> 1 envelope active dry yeast
> ½ cup lukewarm water
> 1 teaspoon sugar
> ¼ cup softened butter
> 1 teaspoon salt
> ¼ cup sugar
> 1 egg, 2 egg yolks, slightly beaten together
> 2¾ cups sifted all-purpose flour, approximately
> ½ cup golden seedless raisins
> ½ cup thinly sliced citron and orange peel, mixed

Mix the yeast with the lukewarm water and 1 teaspoon sugar and let stand a few minutes. Mix the butter, salt, sugar, and the egg and egg yolks. Add the yeast and butter mixtures to the flour and stir the dough until it is well blended. It should be soft, not stiff, but if it seems too moist to handle, add a bit more flour. Turn it out onto a floured breadboard and knead until it is well blended. Add the raisins and the citron and orange peel and knead them in. Then place the dough in a greased bowl, cover with a clean towel, and put in a warm place (about 80°) until doubled in size. Knead the dough again until it is smooth and place it in a buttered 1-lb. coffee can. Double the recipe for a cake to be baked in a 2-lb. can or in two 1-lb. cans, which I much prefer. Bake in a preheated 350° oven for 30 to 35 minutes, or until a skewer or straw inserted comes out clean.

Serve with coffee, tea, or wine.

◄§ PARIS-BREST

Paris-Brest (not in this case the railway of the same name) is a circle of pâte à chou baked with almond slices on top. This is filled with whipped cream mixed with praline powder*. It may be made ahead and frozen.

1 recipe of pâte à chou (see recipe for gougère* but omit cheese)
¼ cup sliced almonds
2 cups heavy cream, whipped
1 cup praline powder*
½ cup whole strawberries, washed, hulled and dried

Pipe the pâte à chou in a ring on a cookie sheet, using a pastry bag or spoon. Arrange the almonds on the top. Bake in a preheated 400° oven for 10 minutes. Reduce the heat to 350° for 25 to 35 minutes more. Do not remove the pastry from the oven until it is quite firm to touch. Cool. To fill, slice in half horizontally and remove any moist filaments. Mix the whipped cream with the praline powder and fill the bottom half of the pastry with ⅔ of the mixture. Top with the almond-studded half. Place on a serving plate, fill the center of the ring with the rest of the whipped cream and praline mixture, and arrange the strawberries in the center. Serves 4 to 6.

Serve after pork tenderloin with rosemary-scented apricot aspic*; risotto di funghi*; mixed green salad.

ᥱᣠ CHOCOLATE BROYAGE

Halfway between a torte and macaroon, this is a light, sublime dream of a cake rather than a bulky, bunchy affair like what is called birthday cake. It has many names—dacquoise, gâteau, Nuss Schaummasse, and Swiss broyage—and many minor variations in the proportions and in the kind of nuts used. This version has chocolate in the meringue. It is best when used like a batter for drop cookies, but apparently most people like to put it in a pastry bag and squirt it onto a greased and floured cookie sheet. With a filthy-rich butter cream it is called a dacquoise. I prefer to use whipped cream and praline or a chocolate mousse for a filling when making a set piece, and call it broyage.

6 egg whites
¼ teaspoon cream of tartar
pinch of salt
1 teaspoon vanilla
⅔ cup sugar, preferably the extra fine
1 cup finely ground blanched almonds
(or half almonds and half ground hazelnuts)
1 tablespoon cornstarch
¼ cup unsweetened cocoa

Beat the egg whites until they form soft peaks. Add the cream of tartar, salt, and vanilla and stir slightly. Add ⅓ cup sugar, a little at a time, while continuing to beat. Mix the rest of the sugar, ground nuts, cornstarch, and cocoa together and add to the beaten whites, a little at a time, beating after each addition, until all has been added. Outline 3 8-inch circles on a floured and greased cookie sheet (if yours is small, you may need two sheets), using a flan ring or the bottom of a spring-form cake pan as a guide. Fill in the circles with a very thin layer of batter. Traditionally, this is done with a pastry bag and tube, starting at the center and spiraling to the borders; however, you can use the back of a spoon with equally good results. Bake in a preheated 275° oven for 50 minutes to an hour. Remove to a wire rack to cool and dry. They will be crisp and stay so if kept in a tin with a tightly fitted lid. These may also be made as small drop cookies and are delicious plain. Make sure the batter is very thin on the pan. Bake for a shorter time, of course.

To assemble: Put one broyage layer on the bottom of an 8-inch spring-form pan. Spread generously with chocolate mousse* or with whipped cream mixed with praline powder*. Place another of the layers on top and spread that with the mousse or praline mixture and cover with the last layer. This can be topped with more mousse or praline or left plain. Cover with aluminum foil and chill. This can be done the day before for convenience. To serve, remove rim and place the cake with the bottom tin on a glass cake plate. Serves 6 to 8 modestly.

CRISP CHOCOLATE COOKIES

A tender version of chocolate-chip cookies, in which the cookie itself is chocolate too. This is best made with the very tiny chocolate chips now available commercially. Be sure you buy only the *real* chocolate kind.

> ½ cup butter
> ½ cup white sugar
> ¼ cup tightly packed brown sugar
> 3 tablespoons cocoa
> ½ cup real chocolate bits (smallest size)
> 1 cup flour, minus 2 tablespoons
> ¼ teaspoon baking soda
> 1 teaspoon vanilla
> 1 tablespoon light cream

Put the first 4 ingredients in the blender and blend briefly until thoroughly mixed. Pour into a bowl and stir in the rest of the ingredients. Drop by the teaspoonful onto a greased cookie sheet, allowing about 1 inch between the cookies for spreading. Bake in a preheated 350° oven for 8 to 10 minutes, watching carefully. They burn easily. Makes about 30 small cookies.

PAPER-THIN GINGERSNAPS

The British and the Chinese seem to be the only people who treat ginger with great imagination, skill, and respect, although in most countries it is a staple ingredient on the kitchen shelf. A major American cookie manufacturer used to make a thin ginger cookie, but no longer. One can buy English ginger crisps, but it is a real pleasure to make them yourself according to this old-fashioned recipe. A wonderful dividend is the aroma that pervades your kitchen while they are baking.

½ cup sugar
½ cup molasses
½ cup butter
1 teaspoon salt
1 teaspoon fresh, strong powdered ginger
1 teaspoon baking soda
3¼ cups flour (about)

Mix the first 5 ingredients together and cook in a saucepan over medium heat for about 10 minutes. Dissolve the soda in 2 tablespoons boiling water and stir into the hot mixture. Sift in as much flour as possible until dough is stiff. (The texture will vary with the flour, and the moisture in the air.) Roll the dough very thin on a floured board and cut in 2-inch circles. Bake on a buttered, floured cookie sheet at 325° for 10 to 12 minutes, or until crisp. Watch constantly as these cookies burn incredibly easily. The dough may also be rolled in long rolls and frozen uncooked; simply slice thin and bake, allowing a slightly longer cooking time. Makes about 5 to 6 dozen cookies, depending on just how thin the dough is rolled or sliced.

A Reward of Beans

The multicolored, multishaped dried legumes that I somewhat loosely call beans are very beautiful and very well behaved. They are to culinary life what well-tailored tweeds are to one's wardrobe. They last almost forever and they are wonderfully suitable on many occasions.

Among the many kinds of dried legumes, the following are the ones likely to be found these days both in fancy food stores and in supermarkets: kidney beans, Mexican pink beans, the handsome black or turtle beans, the grayish green lentils that make the soup Esau is said to have sold his birthright for, chickpeas (also called garbanzos, and ceci), cranberry or Roman beans, and—very delicate, very expensive, and very difficult to find—the pale green flageolets, a small French kidney bean. Almost all of these can be used interchangeably if you do not mind flouting tradition. Many are also available cooked and canned for instant use.

Although they are even harder to find, I also love small Egyptian lentils that resemble pale orange sequins. I kept a bag of them for personal and sentimental reasons in my kitchen for more than thirty years, and when I recently cooked a few, they were delicious.

I usually keep three or four different kinds of legumes at a time on hand, even though I have a good supermarket right around the corner. This makes me feel that I have a well-stocked larder, and indeed I do. Even in a big city I like the idea of being snug and weather-bound once in a while.

I am most likely to have on hand dark red kidney beans, both dried and canned, to make the Persian red beans in butter or Italian ones with spinach and pignolias, and I also keep some black beans around for soup, and to cook with rum and serve with cold sour cream. The black beans are also the starting point for the spectacular Brazilian dish called feijoada, but I am more apt to make the casserole of black beans that appears in this chapter, which is a much simpler and an equally delicious concoction. Great Northerns I like to have around for traditional Boston baked beans, which do not seem even distantly related to the nondescript canned variety that bears the same name. And large dried lima beans are nice to have on hand.

These sturdy and urbane dishes are good for large parties despite their peasant origin or perhaps because of them. They certainly fit in with our present love for peasant clothes and informal living.

⋙ CASSEROLE OF BLACK BEANS

Black beans are usually met with on American menus as a delicious soup, but they are delectable in many different, attractive ways. Once they had to be started from scratch, soaking and simmering until tender, but black beans may now be found in cans in Spanish American markets. This dish is time-consuming but not in the least complicated. It is a real melting pot to which several European dishes and one Brazilian version have contributed some of their characteristics.

1 lb. dried black beans
1 head of garlic
½ cup beef stock
½ cup red wine
salt, pepper if necessary
1 large or 2 medium chopped onions,
preferably the red sweet ones
3 tablespoons olive oil
2 tablespoons vinegar
1 dry, hot red pepper
salt, black pepper
1 cup sour cream
watercress
3 medium-sized fresh oranges, peeled and sliced thin crosswise,
sprinkled with freshly chopped mint and chilled

Soak the black beans for several hours, or overnight, or use the pre-soaked kind. Drain and simmer in fresh water with the unpeeled head of garlic until tender (about 1½ hours). Remove the garlic and drain. (This may be prepared ahead of time.) Heat the beans in the beef stock and red wine in a 2-quart casserole, adding salt and pepper if the stock needs seasoning. Marinate the onions for half an hour in the oil, vinegar, red pepper, salt, and black pepper. Serve the beans out of the casserole, accompanied by separate bowls of sour cream, watercress, marinated onions, and sliced oranges. Serves 4 to 6.

Serve with tongue or roast loin of pork; hard rolls; strawberry tarts.

✌ᢟ CASSOULET

Despite all the contentious verbal goings-on of culinary purists, it is almost impossible to make a bad cassoulet. Essentially it is a dish of varied meats, roasted separately, and then baked with the beans moistened by the meat juices. The best drippings for this dish come from fatty birds. Geese are traditional because in areas of France they are very plentiful. Here in the United States our plentiful and comparatively inexpensive ducks do very well. One of the meats should be a well-seasoned sausage, and another should be roasted pork or lamb.

When time is short, I sometimes use the canned big Italian beans called cannellini or horticulture beans, adding a roasted rack of tiny New Zealand lamb chops, whatever sausage was at my market, and perhaps a few pork chops. But, as always, a combination of the best ingredients makes the best dish. Obviously, this is not a dish one whips up for two, but it is perfect for entertaining a large group. There must be, of course, a very large pottery or enameled dish in which one can both bake and serve. I often use a shallow 16-inch enameled ironware pot that holds 4 quarts. The crust on the cassoulet is much esteemed. Some stir the crust in and let another crust form, stirring that in, and serve it with a third crust. This is good but not always necessary.

2 *lbs. dried Great Northern beans marked "no soaking necessary"*
or 3 large cans cannellini or horticulture beans
4 tablespoons salt
1 Long Island duckling or 1 turkey thigh and leg
4 lamb shanks
1 lb. Polish, Italian sweet or hot sausage, or cotechino
½ *lb. slab bacon or salt pork, cut in 1½-inch squares, rind and all*
2 cups chopped onions
2 cloves garlic, mashed
2 tomatoes, quartered and seeded
4 cups or more beef stock
1 cup red wine
1 bay leaf
more salt
1½ cups breadcrumbs

Cook the dried beans in 2 or 3 quarts of water with 4 tablespoons of salt until tender. (If the skins curl back when you blow on them, the beans are tender.) Drain well and rinse. Meanwhile, roast the duck or turkey thigh and leg, the lamb shanks, and the sausage, each in separate pans, at 350°, until tender—the times will vary. Some sausage may require boiling instead of baking, so check with your butcher when buying it. When the separate pieces are tender, remove from the oven and save all the drippings for the cassoulet. Cut the various pieces of duck or turkey, lamb, and sausage into 2½-inch chunks, keeping the bones for soup or discarding them if you must. Put the meat chunks in the bottom of the baking dish and cover with the drained beans. Combine all the other ingredients except the breadcrumbs. Pour over the beans and meats, tucking the pieces of bacon or pork in amongst the beans. Add more beef stock if necessary so that the liquid covers the beans. Sprinkle the top with the breadcrumbs and sprinkle the breadcrumbs with the drippings. Bring the cassoulet to a boil on top of the stove, then bake in a preheated 350° oven for 1¼ hours. Serves 10 to 12.

Serve with mixed green salad; fresh fruit; red wine.

ᴇᶳ CHILE CON CARNE

I have tried this with both cubed beef and ground, but I prefer the former, cooked with beans American fashion.

3 scallions, tops and bulbs chopped
2 tablespoons olive oil
1½ lbs. round steak, cut in 1-inch squares
¼ cup fat from steak, chopped
salt
1½ teaspoons cumin seed
chili powder—1 to 5 tablespoons (get the best)
1 clove garlic, chopped
2 cups hot water
2 1-lb. cans red kidney beans

Cook the scallions in a large skillet in olive oil until they are yellow. Add the meat, fat, salt, and cumin. Stir until the meat is brown, then add chili powder and garlic. Cook uncovered over medium heat about 10 minutes. Add the hot water and stir. Put the mixture into a deep casserole, add the kidney beans, cover, and cook in a 350° oven for 40 minutes. Serves 4 or more.

Serve with escarole salad with a little olive oil and salt (no vinegar— the chile is hot enough); tortillas (if available); beer.

◄§ FLAGEOLETS AND SAUSAGES WITH AIOLI

Lentils may be used instead of flageolets for a more frugal dish.
Aioli is an oil-based sauce made with garlic. A good brand of mayonnaise, *not* salad dressing, with the juice of 2 cloves of garlic stirred
in, could be used, but it will not be as good as that made in a blender
or by hand.

> *1 lb. flageolets, soaked and simmered until tender*
> *1¼ cups beef stock*
> *¼ cup red wine*
> *salt, pepper*
> *1 lb. Italian sweet sausages, sautéed briefly in oil*
> *aioli**

Put drained, cooked flageolets in a 2-quart casserole. Mix the
beef stock with wine, salt, and pepper and add to the beans. Top
with sausages, and bake covered in a 350° oven 30 minutes. Serve the
aioli at room temperature in a separate bowl. Serves 4.

*Serve with red oak-leaf lettuce with oil-and-lemon-dressing; poppy-
seed rolls; cream puffs (see recipe for gougère* but omit the cheese)
with coffee-flavored whipped cream.*

◄§ FLAGEOLETS À LA CRÈME

This goes very well with a smoked mutton leg, or mutton ham.
I became so curious about the taste of such a thing when I first read
about it that I almost added to New York's pollution problem by
smoking a leg of lamb on a piece of concrete I fondly call my terrace.
Luckily, and just in time, I read in *The New Yorker* about a smoke-
house in upstate New York which would deliver a smoked mutton
anywhere. Naturally, it is simpler and less expensive to serve a
regular ham or a dish like parsleyed ham*, but that mutton roast
was a special treat.

> *2 tablespoons butter*
> *1 14-oz. can (or bottle) flageolets with 3 tablespoons of the juice*
> *½ cup heavy cream*
> *1 teaspoon flour*
> *salt*
> *chopped parsley*

Heat the butter with flageolets and their juice. Mix the cream and flour together and add to the flageolets. Bring to a boil for a minute or two, just enough for the cream to thicken slightly. Remove, salt to taste, and serve sprinkled with the chopped parsley. Serves 4 to 5.

Serve with mutton ham (see above) or parsleyed ham*; orange and black-olive salad*; frozen Alexanders*.

✑ KIDNEY BEANS AND RED WINE

Any good red wine, domestic or imported, will do here, and we like to serve the same wine before, during, and after dinner.

> *3 small scallions, tops and bulbs chopped*
> *½ green pepper, seeded and chopped*
> *1 cup diced cooked ham*
> *3 tablespoons butter*
> *1 6-oz. can Italian tomato paste*
> *1 cup red wine*
> *salt, pepper*
> *2 1-lb. cans kidney beans, drained*
> *8 bacon strips*

Sauté the scallions, green pepper, and ham in butter. Stir the tomato paste into the wine and add the salt and pepper. Stir into the ham mixture and cook 5 to 10 minutes over a medium heat. Put the kidney beans and the ham-wine sauce into a buttered 2-quart casserole and cover with bacon strips.   Bake for 30 minutes in a 350° oven, or until the bacon is crisp.   Serves 4 or more.

Serve with escarole with French dressing; Italian bread sticks.

⋐§ ITALIAN RED KIDNEY BEANS WITH SPINACH AND PIGNOLIAS

A visually and texturally appealing dish that may be served as a hearty one-dish meal with the addition of some crumbled bacon, or pieces of ham, or as a colorful side dish needing only the briefest cooking.

⅓ *cup olive oil*
2 fat cloves garlic, minced
2 10-oz. packages frozen chopped spinach, thawed,
or 2 lbs. fresh steamed spinach, drained and chopped
⅓ *cup pignolias or pine nuts*
salt, pepper
1 large can red kidney beans, drained
6 sliced, cooked, crumbled strips of bacon (optional)

Cook the garlic and spinach briefly in the oil.   Add the pignolias and seasonings, and then the beans.   Heat thoroughly and serve with bacon crumbled on top if you aren't serving the beans with ham. Serves 4 to 6.

Serve with broiled ham; hot sesame seed rolls; frozen pineapple chunks, or, for the energetic, fresh pineapple; paper-thin gingersnaps*.

✑ PERSIAN RED BEANS WITH BUTTER SAUCE

One usually thinks of beans as they are baked in New England, combined with rice in the South and the Caribbean, or highly seasoned with chili in the Southwest. In Iran, however, red beans are traditionally cooked and served in this delicate and savory way, according to Davoud Yonan, an artist who was born there when it was still called Persia. He says that this is better made with buffalo butter because it is more delicate than cow's butter. To be authentic the yogurt should be dried in balls in the sun, then pounded in a mortar with water added a little at a time until a smooth paste is formed. However, plain cow's butter and commercial plain yogurt taste very good. The menu below includes the traditional watercress salad for a spicy accent, but adds a baked slice of ham and open fruit tarts.

1 lb. dried red kidney beans
(or 2 cans without sauce, well drained)
2 medium-sized onions, chopped
2 plump cloves garlic, chopped
1 stick (¼ lb.) butter, preferably unsalted
salt, pepper
paprika

Soak the dried beans overnight, drain, and simmer in fresh water to cover until tender (1 to 2 hours). Drain. The Persians mash the beans slightly, but I rather like the plump, individual look of the whole bean. Sauté the onions and garlic in the butter until pale yellow and translucent, but not brown. Add the well-drained beans, salt, pepper, and paprika and heat together briefly. This may be done in a casserole and kept in the oven until wanted. Serve with a crisp bowl of watercress and a fat pitcher or bowl of yogurt on the side. If this is used for a buffet supper, serve with a whole or half ham. Serves 4.

Serve with thick slice of ham, baked; yogurt; watercress (no dressing); cornmeal muffins; open-faced blueberry tarts; coffee.

⇜ LIMA BEANS BAKED IN SOUR-CREAM SAUCE

The large dried lima beans are so beautiful in shape—if not in color—that they inspired Elsa Peretti to shape them in silver as part of her intriguing series of sculptured jewelry. Equally intriguing is this recipe.

1 lb. dried large lima beans, soaked and simmered until tender,
or 2 1-lb. cans cooked large lima beans, drained
2 tablespoons maple syrup or ⅓ cup brown sugar
1½ teaspoons dry English mustard
½ pint sour cream
salt, pepper
6 strips bacon, cooked and crumbled,
or 4 slices thin ham, cut into small squares
½ teaspoon thyme and rosemary, mixed

Put the drained beans in a 2-quart casserole. Make a paste of syrup, mustard, sour cream, salt, and pepper and add it to the beans, stirring gently. Sprinkle the top with ham or bacon and the herbs. Bake in a 350° oven for 20 minutes—or longer if you want another drink. Serves 4.

Serve with watercress, grapefruit segments, and oil-and-vinegar dressing; hot corn muffins; lemon mousse*.

A Gratitude of Birds

A live chicken is (to me at least) a silly bird, fit only to lay eggs. A duck, on the other hand, is a handsome bird, but pretty noisy and not a very efficient egg layer, judging from the ducks I remember when I was young. Turkeys are impressively big, though not much more interesting than chickens in terms of personality.

But what wonderfully different thoughts these birds inspire when they are killed and dressed for cooking. Even though poultry is relatively plentiful and cheap, there is a festive feeling about "a hot bird and a cold bottle," and in many lands they are still traditional holiday fare. Poultry is suitable for all the medical diets I know about and does not affront any religious beliefs except those that require vegetarianism. Best of all, the choice of cooking methods is intoxicating and limitless.

Brillat-Savarin in his *Physiology of Taste* recognized the amazing adaptability of these birds when he said, "Poultry is for the cook what canvas is for the painter, or the cap of Fortunatus is for the conjurer; it is served to us boiled, roasted, fried, hot or cold, whole or cut up, with or without sauce, boned, skinned, stuffed and always with equal success."

⁂ CAPILOTADE OF ROAST FOWL

More than ten years ago, when I first came across this recipe, I did not know what "capilotade" meant. It is just a French culinary term for a kind of hash, which I might have guessed of such a Francophile as Thomas Jefferson, whose recipe this is said to be.

3 cups leftover roast fowl or a rotisserie chicken, boned and diced
2 tablespoons butter
1 plump clove garlic, minced
1 tablespoon chopped fresh herbs, possibly basil, marjoram, and
mint, or ½ teaspoon dried oregano
1 tablespoon flour
1 cup chicken gravy or broth
⅓ cup white wine

Simmer all the ingredients together for 10 to 15 minutes.   Serves 4.

Serve over waffles; and with raw celery stuffed with Roquefort cheese.

⋐ BRANDIED CHICKEN

Elegant and simple.

¼ cup butter
2 cloves garlic, minced
1 tablespoon good curry powder (see page 176)
1 2½-lb. chicken, cut up
1 cup heavy cream
2 jiggers brandy or rum
salt, pepper

Melt the butter in a heavy skillet and cook the garlic until barely colored and discard it.   Add the curry powder to the butter, stirring until your kitchen is filled with an enticing aroma.   Add the chicken pieces and brown on all sides in the mixture.   Transfer to a casserole with all the juices from the pan.   Add the cream, brandy, salt, and pepper.   Cover and bake in a preheated 350° oven for 35 to 40 minutes, or until the meat is tender when pricked with a fork.   This may also be cooked in a skillet on top of the stove if you prefer.   Serves 4.

Serve with buttered rice mixed with good-sized pieces of pimiento;
raw mushroom salad* with watercress; French bread; apricot soufflé*.

৵ঔ PARSLEYED CHICKEN

Some of the charm of the old-fashioned pressed chicken with some of the color and flavor of parsleyed ham*. It is served in wedges or slices and looks best on a glass platter or bowl of a dark solid color.

1 envelope unflavored gelatin
3 cups strong chicken broth (not cubes)
2 tablespoons tarragon vinegar
salt, freshly ground black pepper
1½ cups finely chopped parsley
3 cups diced or sliced cooked chicken (see following recipe)
2 or 3 preserved kumquats, slivered

Soften the gelatin in ¼ cup cold water and dissolve in 1 cup of boiling chicken broth. Let cool and add the rest of the broth, the tarragon vinegar, salt, pepper, and parsley. Arrange a layer of half the chicken on the serving dish. Pour on enough of the parsleyed broth to cover the meat and put it in the refrigerator to jell. When the glaze is slightly firm, add the remaining chicken and cover it with the rest of the parsleyed broth. If the broth has stiffened too much to pour, warm it slightly over a low heat. Arrange the slivered kumquats in a pleasing design and chill until firm. Serves 4 to 6.

Serve with spoon bread*; Persian mäst*; glazed oranges*; macaroons*.

৵ঔ POACHED CHICKEN

When a recipe calls for cooked chicken, this is a basic, time-honored way to prepare it.

1 5½–6 lb. fowl, plus the gizzard, heart, and neck
2 carrots, trimmed, peeled, and cut in 2-inch lengths
1 onion, quartered
2–3 stalks of celery, cut into 2-inch pieces
1 clove garlic, crushed

1 *tablespoon peppercorns, crushed*
¼ *cup parsley clusters*

Put all of the ingredients in a large, deep pot with water to cover. Bring to a boil. Cover, turn down heat to a simmer, and cook covered for 50 minutes to an hour until thoroughly tender. Remove from the heat and let the chicken cool in the broth. When it is cool enough to handle, remove the chicken from the broth. Pull off the skin and take the meat from the bones. Cut the meat into 1-inch dice and put in plastic containers in the refrigerator if you plan to use it within a day or two. If it is to be used later, cover it tightly and freeze. Strain the broth remaining in the kettle into a fresh saucepan. Bring to a boil and cook until it is reduced by half. Put into plastic containers and keep in the refrigerator or freezer to use in recipes calling for rich chicken broth. Makes about 5 cups diced chicken.

⋖§ CHICKEN BREASTS WITH STRING BEANS AND GINGER

Fresh ginger root can always be found in Chinese food stores, but in these days of culinary sophistication it is often sold in vegetable and fruit stores and even in some supermarkets.

½ *teaspoon thyme*
¼ *teaspoon leaf sage*
⅓ *cup flour*
2 *lbs. chicken breasts*
3 *tablespoons butter*
1 *small onion, sliced thin*
1 *lb. fresh green beans, frenched, or 1 10-oz. package frozen*
1 *small piece fresh ginger root, finely chopped,*
enough to make a tablespoonful

Mix the thyme and sage with the flour and dredge the chicken breasts. Sauté them in butter in a skillet until brown on both sides (about 5 minutes). Place the chicken breasts in a shallow buttered casserole. Brown the onion in the butter remaining in the skillet and transfer to casserole. Thicken the juices in the skillet with the rest of the seasoned flour and thin with 1½ cups water, whisking constantly. Add the green beans to the casserole, sprinkle with chopped ginger, and pour sauce over all. Bake in a 350° oven for 35 minutes. Serves 4.

Serve with romaine lettuce with blue-cheese dressing; Norwegian thin bread; lemon pudding.

ᥬ CHICKEN BREASTS WITH TARRAGON

Often the simplest way of preparing a dish is the best one, as in this elegant concoction. I prefer to skin and bone the breasts myself, since it is very easy to do. I use tarragon vinegar bottled with the leaves if I don't have any fresh tarragon at hand.

8 chicken breasts, skinned and boned
¼ cup melted butter
⅓ cup tarragon vinegar with 2 tablespoons chopped tarragon leaves
1 teaspoon dry English mustard
salt

In a large skillet sauté the chicken breasts in the butter for a few minutes until lightly browned on both sides. Mix together the vinegar, leaves, dry mustard, and salt, and pour over the chicken breasts. Cover and put into a baking dish and bake in a 350° oven until tender (30 to 40 minutes). If the juice boils down, add a little more vinegar mixed half and half with water. Serves 4 to 6.

Serve with kumquats and cream cheese*; spaetzle* with buttered crumbs; Bibb lettuce with cream dressing*; praline soufflé*.

ᴥ PERSIAN CHICKEN
WITH POMEGRANATE SAUCE

This is one of the most beloved Persian chicken dishes which they serve as a sauce for chelo, their traditional way of cooking rice. Inasmuch as pomegranates in the United States are not very juicy and are not always available, I have used grenadine syrup, which is made of pomegranate juice, with a can of condensed orange juice. It isn't authentic, but it tastes fine.

1 tablespoon softened butter
¼ teaspoon poultry seasoning
salt, freshly ground black pepper
1 2½ lb. chicken cut up for frying
½ cup chopped onions
3 tablespoons butter
2 tablespoons tomato paste
2 cups walnuts, chopped
3½ cups water
½ teaspoon cinnamon
2 tablespoons lemon juice
3 tablespoons grenadine syrup
1 6-oz. can frozen condensed orange juice (undiluted)

Mix the butter and poultry seasoning with a pinch each of salt and pepper, and rub it lightly on the skin side of the pieces of chicken. Bake in a preheated 350° oven for 35 to 45 minutes. Remove from the oven and keep warm. Sauté the onions in butter until golden brown. And the tomato paste and cook, stirring, for 3 or 4 minutes. Add the walnuts to the onions and cook over medium heat about 5 minutes more. Stir constantly, being careful not to burn the walnuts. Add the water and the rest of the seasoning—cinnamon, lemon juice, grenadine syrup, and orange juice. Cover and cook over low heat for about 35 minutes. Taste the sauce and add a teaspoon or more of sugar if necessary. Add the pieces of chicken and simmer covered 20 to 25 minutes more until chicken is tender and well blended with sauce.   Serves 4 to 5.

Serve with rice; watercress with vinaigrette dressing made with lemon; crème brûlée*.

~ SWEDISH CHICKEN SOUP WITH CHICKEN QUENELLES

A very elegant but simple way to prepare chicken soup and dumplings.   In Norway it is called Queen Soup.   The chicken quenelles or dumplings must be made a little ahead of time so that they can be chilled enough to handle easily.

CHICKEN QUENELLES

2 cups diced raw chicken breast
6 tablespoons melted butter
2 eggs
1 tablespoon heavy cream or sour cream
1 teaspoon salt

SOUP

4 egg yolks
⅓ cup light cream
¼ cup sherry
6½ cups boiling hot chicken broth, homemade
chicken quenelles

Put the diced chicken meat in a blender (or put several times through a meat grinder using the finest blade) with the melted butter, eggs, cream, and salt.   Blend until velvety smooth.   Chill until firm enough to make into small oval balls that will hold their shape.   To make the soup itself, blend the egg yolks, cream, and sherry briefly. Pour into a warm soup tureen and keep warm in a low oven or on the back of the stove.   Add the seasoned hot chicken broth slowly, beating with a whisk.   Use a teaspoon to shape the quenelles and drop them into rapidly boiling salted water.   Simmer for 8 to 10 minutes and remove with a slotted spoon.   Add to the soup in the tureen and serve.   Serves 6 to 8.

Serve with roast fillet of beef; broiled mushroom caps; dried-fruit compote.

DRIED-FRUIT COMPOTE

dried apricots, peaches, and pears
white wine
orange rind, grated
pine nuts

Soak the dried fruits in white wine to cover and leave for several days.   Serve sprinkled with the grated orange rind and pine nuts.

⮧ ROAST TURKEY, CHINESE STYLE

This manner of roasting a turkey takes much less time than the conventional methods, and the bird becomes a beautiful mahogany color, full of juice and flavor.   A pork loin or a pot roast may be successfully cooked in the same way.   You must have a large, deep roasting pan with a tight cover, the size of the pan depending on the size of the turkey.   The boiling liquid may be refrigerated and used several times.

1 turkey, 12–15 lbs.
3 cups soy sauce
1½ cups sherry
2 tablespoons sugar
4 large slices fresh ginger
or 2 tablespoons chopped preserved ginger
3 scallions
1½ tablespoons salt

Truss but do not stuff the turkey. Bring 9 cups of water to a boil with the seasonings in the roasting pan on top of the stove. Add the turkey and continue to boil briskly for 35 to 40 minutes, covered, turning over from time to time, since the juice will not cover the turkey. Pour the juice off, strain, and save. Bake the turkey uncovered in the same roasting pan in a 500° oven for 45 to 50 minutes, basting with a little juice every 20 minutes and turning over until well browned. Remove the pan from the oven and let stand about 10 minutes or so before serving and carving. Combine any remaining juices with the boiling liquid and store in the refrigerator.

A 5-pound chicken will need to be boiled for only 15 minutes, then let it steep for 20 minutes in the liquid before draining and roasting. Bake at 500° for 15 minutes, basting every few minutes. For the boiling liquid you will need 3 cups of water, 1 cup of soy sauce, 1 tablespoon sugar, ½ cup sherry, 1 slice fresh ginger, and 1 scallion.

Serve with cranberries in apricot brandy*; corn-bread stuffing, baked separately; assorted relishes; ripe, green olives; celery stalks.

CORN-BREAD STUFFING (BAKED SEPARATELY)

1 batch plain corn bread, crumbled into large pieces
2 slices white bread, diced
2 cups turkey broth
¼ cup melted butter
3 cups chopped celery and onions, about half and half
salt, freshly ground black pepper
4 eggs

Mix all the ingredients together in the order given and put them into a large, shallow, buttered oven-proof dish. Bake in a 350° oven about 1 hour, or until brown and puffy. Serves 6 or more.

ᴥ§ VITELLO TONNATO

This is not a purist's version by any means, because turkey breast is used instead of veal roast and because it is baked instead of being braised in a liquid. A way of combining both techniques for either turkey or veal is to bake the seasoned meat wrapped in foil. This is a good party dish because it may be prepared at least a day ahead and everyone seems to like it.

1 piece of turkey breast, about 3 lbs.
olive oil
1 tablespoon fresh tarragon, chopped, or 1 teaspoon dried
1 small onion, quartered
salt, pepper
1 3½-oz. can tuna fish
2 anchovy fillets
juice of 1–2 lemons
⅔ cup more olive oil
¼ cup drained capers
freshly ground black pepper

Put the turkey breast in a baking pan to fit. Rub olive oil all over the meat and sprinkle with chopped tarragon. Tuck the onion quarters around the breast, and sprinkle generously with salt and pepper. Bake in a preheated 400° oven for about 1½ hours, or until tender when pricked with a fork. Let cool.

Put the tuna fish, anchovy fillets, lemon juice, and a bit of the olive oil in the blender. Blend until mixed, then gradually add the rest of the olive oil and any drippings from the turkey pan, blending as you pour. The sauce should be thin, so add more olive oil if it seems too thick to pour easily. Slice the turkey breast and arrange the pieces in a shallow dish about 2½ inches deep in overlapping circles. Pour the sauce over them and sprinkle with the capers and the freshly ground black pepper. Chill until ready to serve. Serves 6 to 8.

For a dinner, serve with a mixed green salad; hot curried fruit casserole*.

◄§ PEPPERIDGE FARM TURKEY PUDDING

Naturally the very best way to eat cold roast turkey is in the
kitchen, pulling it greedily from the bones with your fingers, but
this is a good, slightly more formal method, and a delightfully quick
one to prepare. The kumquats give the same acid emphasis as
cranberries, but they add a sharp and different aroma and flavor.

12 slices roast turkey (or duck or chicken)
12½-oz. jar preserved kumquats, drained and sliced
(reserve the juice)
1 8-oz can small boiled onions (reserve the juice)
1 package Pepperidge Farm herb-seasoned stuffing
4 eggs
1 cup milk

Place the slices of turkey in four deep individual greased casseroles
or one large one. Divide the kumquats and onions into four parts
and arrange on the turkey slices. Mix the stuffing with the whole
raw eggs, half the juice from the kumquats, the juice from the onions,
and milk. No extra seasoning is needed. Pour the stuffing batter
on top of each casserole and bake in a 350° oven for 35 minutes,
or until firm. Serves 4.

Serve with wilted spinach salad with bacon dressing; lemon granita*.

An Entertainment of Breakfasts

Breakfast was an affront to me when I was young. I did not want any food of any kind thrust at me when I first woke up, though occasionally I would accept a glass of orange juice. I still feel pretty much the same way. I like to have my first cup of coffee along with a croissant or crumpet in utter quiet and privacy before I face whatever the day may bring.

But a late, leisurely Sunday breakfast is one of the best of occasions for entertaining and being entertained. People are relaxed then, having had time to recover from the tensions and fast pace of the week. Even the planning is fun—designing the menu, preparing the dishes that can be made ahead, selecting the mats, napkins, and plates that will give the table color and display the food most attractively.

Most of my friends seem to enjoy champagne for their Sunday breakfasts. Even the worldly ones relish the deliciously decadent and festive feeling that champagne inspires. Some, like me, prefer still white wine, and a few of my family and friends like a more emphatic jolt, a Bloody Mary or a mint julep.

I like keeping the food simple but somehow special. Bread from a good bakery or made at home transcends the run of the mill by being served with unsalted butter and an array of sweets—honey, strawberry jam, ginger marmalade, or what you will. Many kinds of fruit desserts are also appropriate for a special breakfast. One of my favorites and one of the most beautiful is a ripe honeydew melon cut in wedges, each piled high with blueberries and straw-berries. Another crowd pleaser, which is fitting to the hour, is grape-fruit Alaska. The recipes for this and other similar dishes are found throughout the book. Light luncheon dishes—especially those fea-turing eggs and cheese—can be made quickly and easily and make a

57

welcome change from plain breakfast fare.

One of the best ways to become thought of as a fine cook is to serve coffee distinguished for its flavor and clarity. I am an inveterate coffee lover. Coffee was the first and loveliest flavor I knew and remembered, in ice cream, in cambric coffee (about a tablespoon of liquid coffee to a cup of sweetened hot milk, I imagine), and in coffee Bavarian cream—and it still is. Perhaps being given these at my grandmother's house might have had something to do with it. There was love and warmth and understanding there. And though I came rather late to coffee as a beverage, it is very important to me.

There are many ways to make a good cup of coffee. The worst (aside from instant coffee) is in a percolator, which boils or steams the coffee, making it somewhat bitter. The best I have found is the drip method, preferably with a filter, although one can make superb espresso in a Vesuviana nonelectric machine. There are several good blends of canned coffee on the market, but I prefer to grind my own beans in a French electric grinder. Since I have never settled on a single house blend of my own, I happily continue to experiment with different blends or varieties that I find at various shops in my neighborhood or bring back with me from my travels. By far my favorite is a bean from Haiti, but it isn't easy to find it in this country. There are certain hazards involved in buying coffee beans, since there is no guarantee that the coffee will taste as good as it smells, or even that it is what it is said to be. Recently, several reputable distributors advertised Jamaica Blue Mountain coffee in their catalogues, until one of them, the only importer of the real Blue Mountain, yelled aloud in print and silenced the rest. But this search for the best coffee bean is an enjoyable and relatively inexpensive way to live dangerously, even at today's prices.

My proportions for making coffee are: 2 tablespoons of ground coffee to ¾ cup of water for each cup, although it can be made stronger or weaker according to individual preference or tolerance. The water should not be allowed to come to a full boil before it is poured over the coffee; some people say it should reach a temperature of 180°, others say 200°, but since I find it inconvenient to take the temperature of boiling water, I simply listen to the water and remove it from the heat when it starts making active noises.

✑ GRAPEFRUIT ALASKA

A light and happy ending for a dinner or the highlight of a late and leisurely breakfast. It is not difficult to prepare and it always pleases those who like their sweets to have a certain panache.

4 grapefruits, cut in half
¼ teaspoon cream of tartar
6 egg whites
¾ cup confectioners' sugar, sifted
½ pint sherbet (lemon, orange, or pineapple),
or vanilla ice cream

Separate the segments in the grapefruit halves and cut around the skin, removing the core and the seeds. Chill until needed. Make a meringue by mixing the cream of tartar with the egg whites and whipping them until foamy. Add a little sugar and whip some more until all the sugar has been used and the whites are glossy and stiff. Mound a spoonful of sherbet or ice cream in the center of each grapefruit, smoothing it out to the sides. Spread the meringue on top of each half, being careful to reach the edges. Bake for 5 minutes in an oven preheated to 450° and serve immediately. This is a last-minute operation, so arrange to have one of the guests help bring the main-dish plates out. Serves 8.

For breakfast, serve with Black Forest ham; Swedish omelet* with lingonberry preserve; lots and lots of coffee.

⚜ LAKS PUDDING

This laks (or salmon) pudding, delicate in color, flavor, and texture, was a specialty of Rolf Svensson, chef of the Swedish American Line's *Stockholm*. It should be served warm.

4 thick slices smoked salt salmon (6 x 2 inches)
about 1 cup milk
4 medium-sized boiled potatoes, sliced
2 eggs
1½ cups light cream
2 sprigs fresh dill, chopped, or ½ teaspoon dried dill

Soak the salmon in milk to cover for several hours or overnight. Drain it and stand slices on end in a buttered casserole, alternating with potato slices. Beat the eggs and add the cream to them. Stir until the mixture is well blended. Sprinkle the dill on the salmon and potatoes and pour in the egg mixture. Bake in a preheated 350° oven for 20 to 25 minutes. Serves 4.

Serve with a pale green cucumber salad that complements the pale pink of the pudding; French bread; fruit and cheese.

⚜ BLACK CHERRIES WITH NUTS AND CREAM

Serve first for Sunday breakfast or as a simple and delectable ending to a meal.

2 lbs. large fresh Bing cherries
or 1 large can pitted Bing cherries, drained
¼ cup powdered sugar
1 cup (¼ lb.) shelled unsalted hazelnuts
1 jigger kirsch
1 cup heavy cream, lightly whipped

If using the fresh cherries, pit them or not as you are inclined. (It's tedious but worth it.) Mix with the sugar (but not if you use the canned cherries). Add the hazelnuts, kirsch, and lightly whipped cream. The hazelnuts, if they are the right size, can be stuffed into the pitted cherries but this is not necessary. Mix together and chill a half hour or more before serving. Serves 6 to 8.

As a dessert, serve after Hungarian chicken*; rice pilaf; beet and endive salad with walnuts*.

ᴥᶓ PITCHER OF PEACHES IN WINE OR CHAMPAGNE

This is one of the simplest, freshest, and most charming ways to serve wine and fruit. It looks best in a glass pitcher large enough to hold a bottle of wine and the required number of peaches, one for each person.

Peel the peaches by first dropping them in boiling water for a few seconds. I like the decorative look of a whole peach, but some people prefer them sliced. Pour in the wine, which may be champagne or a dry white wine. Serve the wine during the meal and the peaches for dessert. I generally use a white wine for dinner and champagne for Sunday brunch.

Serve with Swedish omelet*; popovers; coffee.

ᴥᶓ CRUMPETS

A delicate and lovely bread for breakfast or tea, crumpets are usually first encountered by Americans in English novels or in their sturdier and debased counterpart, the English muffin. Real crumpets are cooked in 3-inch flan rings in a skillet on top of the stove. Acceptable rings can be made from the 6½- or 7-ounce tunafish cans opened at both ends.

1 envelope active dry yeast
½ teaspoon sugar
2 tablespoons lukewarm water (110° to 115°)
1 cup all-purpose flour, sifted
¼ teaspoon salt
½ cup milk
1 egg
5 tablespoons butter, cut into bits (at room temperature)

Sprinkle the yeast over the lukewarm water and sugar in a small bowl and let stand for several minutes, stirring once to dissolve completely. Put the yeast in a warm and unbreezy spot for 4 or 5 minutes more, or until it bubbles up and thickens. (If it doesn't, try another envelope of yeast.) Put the sifted flour and salt in a large bowl and make a well in the center. Pour in the yeast mixture, the milk, and the whole egg. Beat well with a wooden spoon. Add 1 tablespoon of the butter and beat well until you have a smooth soft batter. Drape a towel over the top and put the bowl in a warm draft-free place for about an hour, or until the batter has doubled in bulk.

Meanwhile, clarify the rest of the butter by heating over a low heat without letting it brown. Skim off the foam and pour off the clear butter into a small bowl, discarding the solids at the bottom of the pan. Brush the insides of the five flan rings and the bottom of a heavy 10- or 12-inch skillet with some of the butter. Arrange the rings in the skillet and put the pan over moderate heat. Put about a tablespoon of batter in each ring. The batter will spread out to fill the ring; add a bit more batter if necessary. When bubbles appear in the crumpets and the bottoms turn a light brown, remove the rings and turn the crumpets with a spatula or pancake turner and brown on the other side. Transfer the cooked crumpets to a warm plate and keep warm. Butter the rings and the skillet again and cook the remaining batter. Makes 10 crumpets.

Serve with butter, marmalade, or jam; coffee or tea.

⤚§ EGGS BENEDICT

A deservedly beloved egg dish for a late leisurely breakfast or lunch, this is also a sophisticated American classic. Like all dishes it is only as fine as its ingredients. There are some admittedly depressing concoctions served under that name in restaurants, where the muffins are soggy, the ham soapy tasting, and the sauce a rather peculiar tasting non-hollandaise. With homemade English muffins, fine ham, and good hollandaise, however, it is a perfect dish. Eggs Benedict are easy to make, but with the logistics of getting the hollandaise, eggs, and toast done at the same moment and getting it all assembled, they take a bit of practice.

8 slices cooked ham, cut cardboard thick (the best you can buy),
or good Canadian bacon
6 egg yolks
⅓ cup fresh lemon juice
¼ teaspoon salt
pinch of cayenne pepper
1 cup (2 sticks) melted unsalted butter
4 English muffins or crumpets*, split in half
8 poached eggs

Trim the slices of ham or Canadian bacon into 3-inch circles. Make the hollandaise according to any basic recipe or try this easy blender way. Put the egg yolks, lemon juice, salt, and cayenne in the blender jar; blend for a minute or two, then remove the top and pour in the melted butter while the motor is still going. When the butter is completely absorbed, pour the sauce out of the blender and keep it warm until ready to assemble the dish. Toast the muffin halves and keep them warm. Poach the eggs in a large skillet of simmering water. Meanwhile place the ham circles on the toasted muffin halves on a platter or individual plates, allowing two halves to each person. Remove the poached eggs with a slotted spoon and place one on each muffin half. Spoon the sauce over. Serves 4.

Serve with black cherries with nuts and cream*; orange and green tomato salad; more toasted muffin halves; lots of good coffee.

⋍ SWEDISH OMELET

More substantial than most omelets, and simple to make, this custardy Swedish omelet is ample for Sunday breakfast, luncheon, or supper. It is particularly attractive prepared and served in a decorative oval copper pan or enameled ironware skillet that can go on top of the stove, in the oven, and then onto the table. To be authentic, it should be served with a preserve made of whole lingonberries, which are somewhat like cranberries and obtainable at fine food stores. Any tart jelly or jam, however, tastes good with it.

8 slices bacon, cut in pieces
5 eggs
3 tablespoons flour
½ teaspoon salt
dash of pepper
2 cups milk

Sauté the bacon until crisp. Pour off all the fat except for 2 to 3 tablespoons. Leave the bacon in the pan and keep it warm while you are beating the eggs until they are light and fluffy. Add the flour, beat some more, and then add seasonings and milk, blending well. Pour the egg mixture over the hot bacon and bake in a preheated 375° oven for about 35 minutes, or until puffy and firm. Serve in the pan, accompanied by a separate dish of lingonberries or cranberry preserve. Serves 4.

Serve with grapefruit halves with a dash of port wine; toasted English muffins with jam.

⋍ OMELET WITH SORREL SAUCE

Sorrel is one of the loveliest summer greens, with a fresh sour taste, which explains its common name of sour grass. Sorrel is grown commercially, but there is also a wild green in the eastern United States with the same name, a similar flavor, but a different appearance, with leaves about the same size as white clover. It can be gathered and used the same way, but picking it is a very tedious job.

⅓ cup chopped fresh sorrel
3 tablespoons butter
5 eggs, lightly beaten, at room temperature
salt, freshly ground black pepper

Make the sauce before you start the omelet and keep it warm. Sauté the sorrel in 2 tablespoons of the butter over a low heat until, as the French say, the sorrel is melted. Heat the remaining table-spoon of butter in an 8- or 9-inch skillet until melted and slightly browned. Add the eggs and salt and pepper. Lift the edges of the omelet to let the liquid run down until all the egg is cooked. Flip one half over onto the other half and slide it out onto a warm plate. Pour sorrel sauce over it. Serves 2.

Serve with smoked salmon; croissants; peaches in champagne*.

೫ CHARLESTON SHRIMP BREAKFAST

In Charleston, South Carolina, tiny cold cooked shrimp are served for breakfast with cold tomatoes, hot hominy, and hot biscuits. Sometimes, however, shrimp paste is served instead, a velvety and voluptuous concoction of ground or mashed shrimp and lots of but-ter, chilled long enough for the flavors to lose their individual iden-tities and become something entirely new and good. Shrimp paste is also a superb spread on fresh, hot, very thin toast and served with cocktails or tea.

1½ lbs. shrimp, cooked, peeled, and deveined
¼ lb. butter, melted
pinch of mace
½ teaspoon dry mustard
1 teaspoon lemon juice
salt, pepper
2 tablespoons sherry

Grind the shrimp in a meat grinder, putting it through twice; or put it in an electric blender with the melted butter. (If you use the blender, make half the recipe at a time.) I often like to crumble the shrimp with my fingers, a simple, sensuous, and somewhat unorthodox method. However you proceed, mix the butter and seasonings with the mashed shrimp, pack the mixture in a mold or loaf pan, and chill until needed. This paste can be frozen if it is carefully sealed so that other odors do not work their way in. It will keep safely for several months in the freezer, but after about a month or six weeks the flavor seems to deteriorate, although the paste is still edible.

Serve with cold sliced tomatoes; hominy grits; hot biscuits and butter.

⊷§ CORNMEAL PANCAKES WITH CREAMED CHICKEN

A good light meal, though not too light, for Sunday breakfast, lunch, or a late supper. It is especially felicitous for a late, leisurely breakfast, a time I often choose to entertain.

PANCAKE BATTER

1 cup cornmeal (either yellow or white,
but preferably water-ground)
1 teaspoon salt
1 tablespoon sugar
1 egg
½ cup milk
3 tablespoons melted butter
½ cup flour, sifted before measuring
2 teaspoons baking powder

Mix the cornmeal, salt, and sugar in a bowl and scald by pouring 1 cup of boiling water over the mixture. Beat in the egg, milk, and melted butter. Resift the flour with the baking powder and, with a few brisk strokes, add it to the cornmeal. Heat a small skillet about 5–6 inches in diameter and melt in it a pat of butter until it bubbles over the bottom of the pan. Put in 1 large tablespoon of the cornmeal batter and sauté until its bubbles pop; then turn and cook on the other side. Put the cake aside and keep it warm while you are making the next one. Fill each of these with 1 tablespoon of the creamed chicken mixture (see below) and fold over. Arrange on a small warm deep platter. Cover with more of the sauce and oven-brown briefly before serving.

CHICKEN FILLING

4 tablespoons butter
4 tablespoons flour
1 cup chicken broth
1 cup heavy cream
salt, pepper
2 cups diced cooked chicken (see poached chicken*)
1 jigger (2 oz.) cognac

Melt the butter, blend in the flour, and cook until smooth. Add the chicken broth slowly, stirring constantly until it is thickened and smooth; then add the heavy cream, salt, and pepper. When that is smooth and thickened, add the chicken and the cognac. Serves 4.

Serve with white wine or champagne; strawberry and raspberry granita*; lots of espresso.

⋙ SOPAIPILLAS (FRIED CAKES)

These are the favorite hollow, hot bread of the New Mexicans, and even of those who have tarried only briefly in that fascinating state. They are often eaten with a little honey poured in one of the torn-off corners, but I prefer to eat them with plain butter.

2 cups flour
1 teaspoon salt
2 teaspoons baking powder
2 tablespoons shortening
2 eggs
2–4 tablespoons water or milk
fat for deep frying

Sift the flour with the salt and baking powder. Cut the shortening into the flour with a pastry blender. Beat the eggs lightly and add to the flour mixture. Add enough milk or water to make a medium dough, neither stiff nor soft, and let the dough stand for 30 minutes. Roll out the dough ¼ inch thick, cut into 1½-inch squares, and fry in deep fat heated to 400°. Fry just a few at a time. Push under the fat several times to make sure they are thoroughly cooked. Makes about 20 sopaipillas.

For lunch, serve with parsleyed chicken*; raw mushroom salad*; lemon granita*.

✑ POTATO PANCAKES

A Hungarian friend of mine has lived in Germany and Vienna for several years. She tells me that in these countries potatoes are never simply an accompaniment to the main course; they're a dessert too. This dish is often served with either applesauce or lemon juice and sugar for dessert. When served with a main dish, a finely chopped small onion is added to the batter and, of course, the applesauce omitted.

6 medium-sized potatoes, peeled
3 eggs
salt, pepper
1–2 tablespoons matzoh meal or breadcrumbs
3 tablespoons oil

Grate the potatoes and squeeze them dry in a clean towel. Mix the grated potatoes with the eggs, salt, pepper, and enough bread-crumbs or meal to make a thin batter. Heat the oil until a few drops of water dance when flicked into the pan. Fry a few at a time and drain. Serves 4.

Serve with apricot and horseradish sauce*; Black Forest ham; glazed oranges*.

↩§ KUGULA OR KUGELE

This is a northern European dish that I learned from Polish friends. It is good for what Katharine Whitehorn in her *Bedsitters' Cookbook* calls a potato-shaped space that many people have, though not me. It can be used as a light one-dish meal or for a buffet. It behaves well.

6 to 8 raw medium-sized potatoes, peeled and diced
¼ cup onions, minced or grated
4 or 5 pieces of bacon, fried crisp and crumbled
¼ cup bacon fat
2 eggs
2 tablespoons flour
salt, pepper
sour cream (very cold)

Grate the diced potatoes in an electric blender two at a time with a little water. After grating, drain them well and squeeze in a dish towel, pressing out surplus liquid. Mix all ingredients except sour cream together and put in a shallow flat casserole greased with bacon fat. Bake in a 350° oven for 50 to 60 minutes, until brown and crusty on top. This may be cooked ahead and reheated. Serve with a pitcher of very cold sour cream. Serves 4.

Serve with Caesar salad*; garlic bread; fruit macédoine (sliced fresh fruit marinated in sugar syrup with a jigger of brandy, fruit brandy, or Cointreau).

₰ SCALLOP AND SPINACH QUICHE

A quiche in one of its less stereotyped manifestations. It is fine for Sunday breakfast or other light and gentle meals.

pastry for a one-crust, 9-inch pie
1 lb. spinach, cooked and chopped, or
1 10-oz. package frozen chopped spinach,
cooked and chopped some more
4 eggs
1 cup cream
pinch of nutmeg
salt, pepper
½ lb. bay or sea scallops, sliced thin

Bake the pie shell for 10 to 15 minutes in an oven preheated to 450°. Let it cool slightly. Spread the spinach on bottom of pie shell. Beat the eggs, add the cream, and beat some more. Add the seasoning and scallops. Reduce heat in the oven to 350°. Pour the scallop mixture over the spinach and bake until a knife inserted comes out clean, about 15 to 25 minutes. Serves 4.

Serve with cherry tomatoes; a half pineapple shell, cut lengthwise, filled with sweetened diced pineapple and topped with lemon granita*.

₰ TOMATOES À LA POLONAISE

Most tomato dishes are cooked too long, or else they are too watery or just plain dull. This one is simply and briefly cooked, and it makes even the cottony tomatoes that get to city markets taste edible. When the ones in the market look too dreary to contemplate, however, I use canned tomato quarters. Needless to say, this dish makes ripe country tomatoes taste heavenly.

3 tablespoons butter
⅔ cup finely minced onions
4 firm ripe country tomatoes, cut in halves horizontally,
or a similar amount of drained canned tomato quarters
⅔ cup heavy cream
salt, pepper

Melt the butter in a frying pan. Add the onions. Put the to-matoes, cut side down, in the pan, and sauté over high heat for 5 minutes. Pierce the skin with a fork, turn the tomatoes, and cook them for 5 minutes more. Pour the cream *around* the tomatoes and cook until it comes to a boil. Add salt and pepper. Serves 4.

For lunch, serve with parsleyed chicken*; French bread; Key lime pie*.

A Fascination of Cheeses

I am not quite sure when I first became a turophile, but it was long before Clifton Fadiman coined this lovely word in the fifties to mean a lover of cheeses. There weren't many varieties available where I lived when I was young, but from the first time I read about toasted cheeses in Johanna Spyri's *Heidi* and about Ben's dreams of cheese in Stevenson's *Treasure Island*, I have been fascinated with cheeses of all kinds. I like cheese for breakfast in the Dutch and Danish manner, and as a snack, with fruit, or in sandwiches. In fact, I like it in any way and at any time. Long ago, an urbane and charming man who saw the way to my heart sent me a large crock of Stilton cheese in port wine. Years later, I still love Stilton, though without the wine.

Even in this day of Velveeta and "cheese food," there is an infinite variety of real cheese available, and it can be found in many areas. The cheeses vary in texture and quality, depending on their age and on the way they have been made and handled, so that it is necessary to acquire some knowledge of them before buying. In spite of the increased number of varieties and purveyors, I find that there are fewer experienced cheese handlers who know the exact moment at which cheese reaches its peak. The variety and abundance make up for this to a certain extent but not entirely. Cheese keeps well in the refrigerator, but it should be brought to room temperature before serving. (Allow two or three hours for this.)

To me cheese is best served plain with a crusty loaf of French or Italian bread, along with wine or beer. The English usually accompany cheese with very good crackers, which is a little less messy and easier to manage when you are entertaining a large group. There is something very warmly hospitable about presenting a whole round cheese for people to eat, like the good feeling that emerges when a hearty soup is served in a large tureen.

My taste in cheese tends to change with the years. As more and more cheeses are being imported, I taste, repeat, adopt, and sometimes discard. But I always go back to ones in the Cheddar group—Vermont, Canadian, and English—and I never lose my taste for Cheshire, double Gloucester, the butter Dunlop from Scotland, and nutty Emmenthaler. A delicate ricotta charms me as do the good cream cheeses—Crema Danica, the Swedish hablé, the French petit-Suisse and Boursin. I like most good blue cheeses, but especially the great ones—Stilton, Roquefort, and Gorgonzola. And there are many other fine cheeses too numerous to list. I do not care for the smelly cheeses such as Limburger, Liederkrantz, and Romadur in any of its spellings. There is an Italian cheese called Manteca which is eaten with bread rather than being cooked as are most cheeses from that country. It looks like an edible white croquet ball with a small knob on top, but in fact it is mozzarella with a ball of sweet butter inside. It is delicious simply sliced, horizontally or vertically, and placed on a slice of good bread.

Americans for the most part have not explored the many ways that cheese may be used in cooking. This chapter includes some of the ways I like to use it.

✑§ PIMIENTO CHEESE

I can't think why people buy those gummy, nondescript cheese spreads which are not even inexpensive, when a dish like this one is so good and so simple to make. It pleases sophisticated tastes and delights even the wary and unadventurous.

1 lb. sharp Cheddar cheese, grated
⅔ to 1 cup mayonnaise
1 small can whole pimientos, cut in ½-inch squares

Mix the cheese with the mayonnaise to make a moist, loose mixture. Stir in the pimiento pieces. Keep chilled until ready to serve with thin sliced pumpernickel or rye or what you will. Makes a pint or more, depending upon the moisture.

Serve before broiled lamb chops; pasta with pesto*; cucumber salad; glazed oranges*.

۶§ VOISIN DELECTABLE CHEESE MESS

According to the late Julian Street, the wine expert, this dish was served at the great Voisin restaurant in Paris, which flourished at the time of the Siege of Paris in 1870. The Voisin made gastronomic history by serving and placing on the menu some strange meats from the Paris zoo and such familiar animals as spaniels, rats, and mice. Happily this pleasant cheese spread requires no exotic ingredients, but it is a refreshing alternative to those dreary and unpalatable commercial cheese concoctions.

½ lb. Roquefort or other blue cheese
½ lb. unsalted butter
cayenne pepper to taste

Bring the cheese and butter to room temperature. Beat both together until well blended, smooth, and creamy. Add the cayenne and stir very well. I quite often add to the mixture a jigger of cognac, and I like to make it in two small crocks rather than one large one. It is good with crisp crackers or French bread and keeps well in the refrigerator.

۶§ GOUGÈRE

Pâte à chou is a wonderfully simple beginning for many of the fine dishes in French cookery. It is the unsweetened pastry most frequently encountered as cream puffs, profiteroles, éclairs, or, my favorite of all, gougère, a cheese pastry indigenous to Burgundy but happily found in many other places.

1 cup water
1 stick butter (½ cup)
1 teaspoon salt
1 cup sifted all-purpose flour
4 eggs
1 cup diced Swiss cheese

Put the water, butter, and salt in a large saucepan and bring to a boil. When the butter is melted, remove from heat, stir the liquid, and dump the whole cup of flour in at one time. Stir well until it all comes together in a ball, leaving the sides of the pan clean. Add the whole eggs, one at a time, stirring well after each addition. To make the gougère, add ¾ cup of diced Swiss cheese, reserving the rest of the cheese for the top.

On an ungreased cookie sheet, make a ring of dough about six inches in diameter on the inside circle. You can use a spoon or a pastry bag with a tube that has a large opening. Put the reserved pieces of cheese around the top of the dough. (You can make small puffs by dropping the dough in teaspoonfuls onto the cookie sheet.) Bake in a 325° oven for about 40 minutes until well puffed and golden brown. Poke a knife in here and there to let the moisture out. Turn off the heat. Leave the small puffs in the closed oven for 10 minutes more, large puff for 15 to 20 minutes more.

Serve as a first course before carbonnade; watercress and fennel salad; coffee granita*.*

⤳ TIROPETES (GREEK CHEESE PASTRIES)

Tiropetes are a delectable appetizer for the Greeks and for many Americans as well. Others, like me, think them fine for a light lunch or supper or even for Sunday breakfast. They are made with filo pastry, which is much like strudel dough and may be found in stores with a Mediterranean clientele, and feta, the tangy Greek cheese. Since feta is very salty, some people prefer to use half feta and half pot cheese. Tiropetes can be made in long rolls and cut in slices later, which I prefer, or made in the traditional triangles. They are best served warm rather than piping hot.

3 tablespoons butter
3 tablespoons flour
1½ cups milk
pepper (no salt)
1 egg plus 1 egg yolk
½ lb. feta cheese
½ lb. pot cheese
2 tablespoons chopped parsley or fresh dill
½ lb. filo pastry sheets
1 cup (2 sticks) melted butter

Make a cream sauce by melting the butter and adding the flour. Cook, stirring constantly, for 2 or 3 minutes. Add the milk slowly, whisking after each addition until the sauce becomes smooth and thickened. Season with pepper. Beat the egg and egg yolk together and add about a tablespoon of the sauce. Beat well and add the eggs to the sauce. Stir in the cheeses and the parsley or dill and remove the pan from the heat. Preheat the oven to 400°.

To make tiropetes in long rolls, separate the filo sheets and brush the first few with melted butter. Wrap a moist cloth around the rest. Put half the cheese mixture down the center of the sheets and bring the sides up together and pinch. Turn over so the pinched side is down and place on an ungreased baking sheet. Make another roll with a few more sheets of filo and the remaining ingredients. Bake for 15 to 20 minutes, or until the pastry is golden brown.

To make the triangles, cut the filo sheets into 3-inch strips and keep them moist until used. Brush a few strips with melted butter. Put a teaspoon of the cheese mixture at one end of the strip and fold the corner up into a small triangle. Continue folding until the whole strip is folded. Repeat until all the ingredients are used.

These are smaller and take less time to cook, perhaps 10 to 15 minutes depending on the metabolism of your oven. These may be prepared ahead of time and frozen, then baked when ready to serve. Makes about 48 triangles or pieces.

Serve the large rolls for Sunday breakfast with a salad, say the raw mushroom; peaches in champagne* with lots of extra champagne.*

◆§ SPIEDINI ALLA ROMANA

I rather dislike excessively doughy dishes such as two-crust pies and sandwiches in which there is more bread than filling, so I was delighted when I found this Italian toasted-cheese "sandwich." Chunks of cheese are skewered along with pieces of Italian bread and anointed with an aromatic blend of garlic, olive oil, and anchovies before broiling.

1 long loaf of Italian or French bread, cut in half lengthwise, and then in 1½-inch chunks
1 lb. of mozzarella cheese, cut in chunks
2 cloves garlic, minced
1 cup olive oil
4 anchovy fillets, mashed, or 2 tablespoons anchovy paste

On four skewers alternate hunks of bread and hunks of cheese, pressing them close together. Heat the garlic and olive oil together or let the garlic stand in the olive oil for a while before using. Stir in the anchovy fillets. With a pastry brush paint the skewers of bread and cheese generously with the garlic and anchovy mixture. Put under a preheated broiler until the bread is toasted and cheese is melted, turning occasionally. Slide the "sandwiches" from the skewers onto a warm platter and serve immediately. Serves 4.

Serve with raw spinach salad with hot bacon dressing; wine sherbet.*

⋐ CHEESE SOUP

While I care deeply about many kinds of soup, I come back to this one again and again. Whether I make a bland and velvety smooth soup or a rough one with coarsely chopped onion, celery, green pepper, and heady red chili pepper, it matters not. I am soothed and tranquilized either way.

> *1 large Bermuda onion, chopped fine*
> *2 tablespoons butter*
> *2 tablespoons flour*
> *2 cups beef stock*
> *2 cups milk*
> *2 cups freshly grated cheese, Swiss Emmenthaler*
> *or a good sharp Vermont or Canadian Cheddar*

Sauté the onion in butter until pale yellow. Sprinkle with the flour and stir until it is well blended with the butter and onion. Add the stock slowly and cook until smooth and thick, stirring all the while. Add the milk slowly, stirring, and simmer. Do not boil. Turn the heat down very low, add the cheese, and stir until melted. Serve in mugs. Serves 4 to 6.

Serve with Italian green bean salad*; Irish coffee.

⋐ FONDUTA ALLA PIEDMONTESE

This is my favorite of all cheese fondues, despite the rarity of fresh white truffles in this country. The canned white Italian truffles have only a shadow of the aroma and flavor of the fresh, but still the shadow is good. I have even used the cheaper Algerian truffles during frugal times.

> *1 lb. imported fontina cheese, diced*
> *2 cups milk, approximately*
> *4 tablespoons butter*

5 egg yolks
pinch of white pepper
4 or more white truffles, sliced paper-thin and slivered
or put through a mandoline†
bread chunks

Soak the rich, buttery cheese with milk to cover for 12 hours or more. Put the cheese and milk in an earthenware or heavy enameled saucepan over medium heat. Beat with a whisk or wooden spoon until the cheese has melted. Add the butter, egg yolks, and pepper, stirring constantly until the mixture achieves the thickness of heavy cream. These steps may be completed in the kitchen and the sauce transferred to a fondue dish and kept warm over low heat. Add the slivered white truffles to the cheese and serve with a basket of bread chunks. Serves 1 to 6 as an appetizer, 3 as a main dish.

◈§ CHEESE AND SMOKED-OYSTER SOUFFLÉ

Smoked oysters bear no resemblance to fresh ones except in shape and origin, having an elusive, intriguing flavor that adds a piquant touch to this dish.

3 tablespoons butter
3 tablespoons flour
1½ cups milk
1 cup grated Cheddar cheese
3 eggs, separated
salt, but not much
1 3-oz. can smoked oysters, drained

Melt the butter and blend in the flour. Add the milk slowly, stirring until the sauce is quite thick. Add the grated cheese and cook over a low flame until it is melted. Remove from heat and stir in

† A mandoline is a French kitchen gadget that cuts or shreds foods into neat, long strips.

the egg yolks, salt, and pieces of smoked oysters. Beat the egg whites until stiff, fold them into the mixture, and pour into a buttered casserole with straight sides. Bake in a preheated 350° oven for 45 to 50 minutes, or until the top springs back when *lightly* touched. Serves 4.

Serve with salad of romaine with slices of avocado and a bland French dressing; hot biscuits; blueberry pie.

ᴇ§ BROCCOLI AND CHEESE CUSTARD

This is a simplification of broccoli Mornay and, to my mind, quite as good. It looks particularly attractive cooked and served in a Mexican pottery loaf dish.

1 bunch fresh broccoli, trimmed and broken into florets
or 1 10-oz. package frozen broccoli
3 eggs
⅔ cup milk
1¼ cups grated sharp Cheddar cheese
salt, pepper

Cook the broccoli until tender; drain and place in the bottom of a shallow buttered casserole. Beat the eggs and add the milk, cheese, salt, and pepper; beat until thoroughly mixed, or whirl in a blender, and pour over the broccoli. Set the baking dish in a pan with about 1 inch of water in it. Bake in a 325° oven for about 25 to 30 minutes, or until the top is brown and a knife inserted in the custard comes out clean. This is good hot or cold and may be cooked ahead and reheated in a moderate oven. Serves 4.

Serve with broiled ham slices; salad of escarole, cooked celery cut in 2-inch pieces and marinated overnight in a tart dressing (2½ parts olive oil, 1½ parts vinegar, salt, pepper, and 1 teaspoon capers), and canned pimientos cut in squares; hot poppy-seed rolls; orange-peel ice*.

ᵉᵍ GREEN CHILIES AND CHEESE

An enticing combination, very simple to prepare from ingredients that are usually on hand in the kitchens of those who are addicted to green chilies, as I am.

½ 4-oz. can green chilies, diced
½ lb. sharp Cheddar cheese, diced
2 eggs
1½ cups milk
½ cup flour
1 teaspoon salt

Mix chilies and cheese together in the bottom of a small buttered casserole. Mix the eggs, milk, flour, and salt in an electric blender, or beat the eggs while gradually adding the milk, flour, and salt. Pour over cheese. Bake in a preheated 350° oven for 35 to 40 minutes. Serves 4.

Serve with sliced tomatoes sprinkled with freshly chopped basil; French bread; fresh peach shortcake.

ᵉᵍ GNOCCHI VERDI

These are delicate and absolutely sublime dumplings, if one can properly describe them with such a prosaic term. The Italians are apt to eat them for a first course much as they do with pasta. I prefer to serve them as a side dish with the main course.

1 lb. fresh spinach or 1 10-oz. package frozen spinach
½ lb. ricotta cheese
pinch of salt
2 egg yolks
3 tablespoons grated Parmesan cheese
flour
4 tablespoons butter, melted
more Parmesan cheese

Cook the spinach briefly, squeeze dry, and chop very, very fine. Mix with the ricotta, salt, egg yolks, and Parmesan. Shape into balls the size of walnuts (in the shell of course) and dust lightly with flour. Bring 2 quarts of salted water to a boil in a large saucepan or skillet. Lower a few gnocchi at a time into the water with a slotted spoon. After about three minutes remove the gnocchi, drain on paper towels, and keep warm while you cook the next batch. To serve, drizzle with melted butter and sprinkle with more Parmesan. Serves 4.

Serve with Canadian bacon in one piece; watercress, avocado, and grapefruit salad with oil-and-vinegar dressing; Marlborough apple pie.*

RICOTTA DESSERT

This simple but sophisticated combination is often used to fill dessert cannelloni, but I like it best served in a stemmed dessert sherbet glass with a sprinkling of shaved bitter chocolate. Ricotta looks like cottage cheese but has a subtle and delectable taste of its own.

½ lb. ricotta
⅓ cup heavy cream
2 tablespoons citron
½ teaspoon vanilla
3–4 tablespoons sugar
shaved bitter chocolate or slivered almonds

Mix all the ingredients except the chocolate or almonds, which are sprinkled over just before serving. Chill. Serves 4.

Serve after parsleyed chicken; risotto di funghi*; Bibb lettuce with oil-and-vinegar dressing.*

A Favor of Eggs

One of the most serenely beautiful of all things—whether occurring in nature or fashioned by man—is an egg, at least it seems so to me. There are lovely uncommon eggs from many birds to be seen at the American Museum of Natural History in New York, but to me nothing surpasses a brown egg from a hen. The sculptor Brancusi, who eliminated details in the simple, sweeping beauty of line, never outshone the unadorned perfection of an egg.

A brown egg has a subtly contoured shape, a rich color unlike the painted factory look of white eggs. True, the contents of brown and white eggs are alike in their magical power to thicken sauces (as in mayonnaise, aioli, and zabaglione), to bind and stabilize (as in frozen creams), to clarify (as in soups and old-fashioned boiled coffee), to garnish, to leaven (as in meringues and soufflés and many other dishes). Eggs are also my favorite restorative: 1 cup orange juice, 2 eggs, and a shot or two of Worcestershire sauce buzzed for a few seconds in an electric blender. Eggs are fine cooked alone, or with a few enhancers such as mushrooms, herbs, bits of ham or bacon, and cheese, and they make perfect dishes for light and impromptu meals. As to invisible uses, simply think of soups, hollandaise sauce, fritter batter, soufflés, quiches, custards, and mousses in which eggs play a necessary role. Hard-cooked, they can be used as hors d'oeuvre and in salade Niçoise—the list is endless. And to top it all, an egg is a neat container of protein and just about every necessary nutrient (except for vitamin C) and costs less than a dime.

The only way I do not like eggs prepared is fried. To me frying seems rough treatment for such delicate and delicious protein.

When I was very young, a neighbor who bred pigeons brought me a fresh pigeon egg that was then poached for my supper. It was a memorable occasion, and the image of that tiny egg so neatly cooked still pleases me when I recall it. Another time we found a few hard-cooked duck eggs in our Easter baskets a natural, delicate celadon green. I have seen many duck eggs since but not celadon green ones.

In the old *Gourmet's Almanac* by Allan Ross MacDougal there are intriguing instructions for making a "great auk's egg." Take a large number of hen eggs, anywhere from twelve to eighteen, and separate them. Put the egg yolks in a small bag (plastic perhaps?) and suspend them in boiling water until the yolks are firm. Remove the bag from the water and the eggs from the bag. Put the hard "yolk" in a larger bag with the liquid whites and again suspend in the water until the whites become firm. Then cut the "egg" in half horizontally, devil the yolks and pile back in the halves of egg white and serve it at a lighthearted meal to delight your guests.

My favorite eater in literature is Piero di Cosimo, whom Vasari describes in his *Lives of the Artists.* "Piero was indeed so devoted to his vocation that he forgot himself and his convenience. He allowed himself, for instance, no other food but hard-boiled eggs, and these he cooked only when he had a fire to boil his glues and varnishes. Nor did he cook them six or eight at a time, but by fifties. He kept them in a basket and ate them when he felt hungry. This mode of existence suited him perfectly; any other seemed to him the merest slavery."

❧ PERSIAN OMELET

Most cuisines have a kind of omelet made of eggs cooked with this or that on top of the stove or in the oven. This omelet, well bulked with grapes and scallions and chicken, I always prefer to bake in the oven. It is a good one-dish meal for brunch or supper and can, of course, be varied infinitely. Many egg dishes like this are served lukewarm in the Mediterranean countries and are even taken on picnics.

1 cup white seedless grapes
¾ cup scallions, trimmed and chopped

¼ cup seeded and diced sweet bell pepper or pimiento
1½ cups diced cooked chicken (see recipe for poached chicken*)
⅓ cup chopped parsley
1 cup orange juice
1¼ teaspoons salt
1 teaspoon curry powder
¼ teaspoon cinnamon
freshly ground black pepper
4 eggs, slightly beaten
1 cup plain yogurt

Arrange the white grapes, scallions, pepper, and chicken in a shallow casserole. Put the parsley, orange juice, salt, curry powder, cinnamon, pepper, and eggs into the blender. Whirl briefly and pour into the casserole over the other ingredients. Bake in a preheated 350° oven for 50 minutes to an hour or until the eggs are firm. Serve warm cut into wedges with cold yogurt. Serves 4.

Serve with watercress (no dressing); a good cream cheese; fresh cherries.

ᔰ MESSY EGGS

This name was applied by an admiring young cousin to one of my favorite ways of cooking eggs for unscheduled hungers. If cooked well, scrambled eggs can be more delicate than omelets, with bits of this and that added for substance and flavor. Because this is a method of cooking used in so many countries, I suspect that it may even satisfy a basic human instinct, rather the way finger painting does. In Denmark a dish of eggs cooked this way is called aeggekage; in the Basque country it is a pipérade; in other parts of France, the phrase "oeufs brouillés" refers to the same sort of thing. In Italy it's called a frittata, in Spain (though not in Mexico) a tortilla, and so on. Do not add so much to the eggs that you overwhelm their flavor. Many combinations are good but these are some of my favorites—

> *diced yellow cheese, chopped canned green chilies*
> *crisp crumbled cooked bacon, chopped clams and juice*
> *Chinese oyster sauce*
> *diced, skinned fresh tomatoes, chopped onion*
> *diced Camembert cheese and white wine*
> *diced ham and sautéed sliced mushrooms*
> *diced zucchini, sautéed briefly in olive oil*

Melt a tablespoon of sweet butter in a cold skillet, add ¼ cup of a food combination from the above list (or one of your own), and heat briefly. Break two eggs for each person into a bowl and beat slightly with a fork. Add salt and freshly ground black pepper and whatever other seasoning you feel would enhance the flavors of the combination. The cheese and chilies need none; the bacon and clams would be better for some fresh or dried dill; Chinese oyster sauce could use a little chopped parsley; and the tomatoes and onion perhaps a little dill or basil. The Camembert and wine or the ham and mushrooms need no embellishment, but a little oregano would be good with the zucchini. Put the eggs into the skillet and scramble them lightly over a low flame until they reach the consistency you like. I prefer them moist.

Serve with white wine or champagne; croissants or some other voluptuous bread; tomatoes à la polonaise*; glazed oranges*.

◆§ PIPÉRADE

An amiable Basque dish in which the eggs are hardly visible except as the frothy lift to the vegetable purée. A pipérade is neither an omelet nor scrambled eggs but has a little of the character of both. The bacon is not traditional except as a cooking fat, although a pipérade is often accompanied by thin slices of ham that on its native ground would be the superb ham of Bayonne. I like a good Black Forest ham, prosciutto, or Canadian bacon. Whatever you do, don't serve that soapy-looking boiled ham found in supermarkets.

2 tablespoons olive oil
2 strips bacon, chopped
4 large sweet bell peppers, preferably red,
seeded and cut in squares
3–4 medium yellow onions, chopped
4–5 large tomatoes, peeled, seeded, and chopped
salt, pepper
4–5 eggs

Heat the olive oil and bacon in a skillet and cook the bacon a bit before adding the peppers, onions, and tomatoes. Cook for about 10 minutes, stirring most of the time, until everything seems to melt into a purée. Add salt and pepper and the eggs one by one, stirring briskly. The eggs should not be individually perceptible. Serve 3 to 4.

Serve with lots of French or Italian bread; ham (see above); tossed green salad; some cheese with more of the same bread.

✑ HARD-COOKED EGGS IN SOUBISE SAUCE

A delicate and lovely main course for a light lunch or supper.

2 cups sliced onions
2 tablespoons butter
¾ cup milk or chicken broth
1 tablespoon flour
salt, white pepper
1 tablespoon French prepared mustard
pinch of nutmeg
2 or 3 tablespoons cream
4 hard-cooked eggs, shelled and quartered
dry breadcrumbs
butter

Sauté the onions in the butter until soft. Add the milk or broth and cook for 10 minutes, or until tender. Purée in an electric blender or put through a food mill. Stir in the flour and season with salt and pepper to taste. Cook over a low heat and stir in the mustard and nutmeg. Add the cream, a tablespoon at a time, until the sauce is thick and smooth but not runny. Arrange the egg quarters in a shallow casserole and spoon the sauce on the top. Sprinkle lightly with breadcrumbs and dot with butter. Bake in a 350° oven until lightly browned, about 25 to 30 minutes. Serves 4.

Serve with hot biscuits; watercress salad with sliced cucumbers, oil-and-vinegar dressing; fresh pears and cheese.

✑ PASTEL DE CHOCLO

This Chilean corn and meat pie can be very, very elaborate or relatively simple and frugal, as in this version.

2 medium-sized onions, chopped
2 tablespoons fat, preferably bacon drippings
2–3 cups diced, cooked beef, lamb, chicken, or a combination
1 cup chicken broth
½ cup seedless raisins
1 teaspoon cumin seed
1 teaspoon oregano or marjoram
salt, pepper
20 pitted olives, green, ripe, or stuffed with pimientos
2 hard-cooked eggs
2 beaten eggs
½ cup milk (1 cup if frozen corn is used)
2 tablespoons sugar
1 tablespoon flour
more salt, pepper
1 package frozen corn niblets or 1 can cream-style corn

Sauté the onions in the fat and add the meat and broth, raisins, and seasonings. Simmer 30 minutes, occasionally stirring the mixture, which should be the consistency of mincemeat. Pour into a baking dish and scatter over it the olives and the hard-cooked eggs, sliced thin. Beat the eggs and milk together and add the sugar, flour, salt, pepper, and corn. Pour over the meat and bake in a medium oven 350° for about half an hour until nicely browned. Serves 4.

Serve with Paraguayan corn bread made with any corn-bread mix adding 1 cup coarsely diced onions and 1 cup grated cheese.

৺ BAKED CORN CUSTARD

A long-time favorite and a delight to those meeting it for the first time.

1 tablespoon minced onion
2 leeks, chopped
3 tablespoons butter
3 tablespoons flour
2 cups milk
1 cup grated Cheddar cheese
½ teaspoon marjoram
salt, pepper
1 pimiento, chopped
1 teaspoon sugar
2 7-oz. cans whole-kernel corn
or 1 10-oz. package frozen cut corn (thawed)
2 eggs, slightly beaten
breadcrumbs
more butter

Sauté the onion and leeks in the butter for 5 minutes over a low heat. Blend in the flour and gradually add the milk and cheese. Add the seasonings, pimiento, and sugar and stir in the corn and eggs.

Pour the mixture into a low buttered casserole, sprinkle top with breadcrumbs, and dot with butter. Bake in a 350° oven for 30 to 35 minutes. Serves 4.

Serve with roast pork loin; green salad with French dressing; toasted finger rolls.

◄§ BAKED EGGS WITH CHICKEN LIVERS

This dish is perfect for a Sunday morning when you want to pamper yourself. It can be as rich as you want, and if you like, heavy cream is a fine addition.

> *1 lb. chicken livers, cut in quarters*
> *3 tablespoons butter*
> *8 eggs*
> *½ cup milk, half and half, or even heavy cream*
> *½ teaspoon dried tarragon*
> *salt, pepper*

Sauté the chicken livers for about 8 minutes in butter in a hot skillet, turning occasionally. Divide the chicken livers into four parts and place in individual casseroles. Beat the eggs and milk and add the tarragon, salt, and pepper. Pour over the livers and bake in a 350° oven for about 25 minutes, or until the eggs are set and custardy. Serves 4.

Serve with fresh peaches and cream; hot biscuits with bitter orange marmalade.

◄§ SPINACH SOUFFLÉ

Someone is always being tiresome about spinach. Either you should eat it because it is good for you or you shouldn't because it is bad for you. No one ever seems to say how good it tastes when properly cooked and seasoned.

3 tablespoons butter
3 tablespoons flour
1 cup milk
⅓ cup freshly grated Parmesan cheese
⅛ teaspoon nutmeg (no more)
salt, pepper
3 eggs, separated
1 lb. fresh spinach, washed, dried, and chopped fine,
or 1 10-oz. package frozen chopped spinach (thawed)

Melt the butter, stir in the flour, and cook for a few minutes over a low heat. Stir in the milk, slowly, cooking until smooth and thickened. Remove from the heat, add the cheese, seasonings, and egg yolks, and blend well. Add the chopped spinach. Whip the egg whites until stiff and fold in gently with a rubber spatula. Turn into a greased casserole with straight sides and bake in a 350° oven for 50 minutes or more until the top springs back when lightly touched. Serves 4.

Serve with broiled chicken breasts; tiny new potatoes, boiled and served in their skins with butter and sour cream.

ଐ EGGPLANT SOUFFLÉ

Eggplant, which is one of the most beautiful of all vegetables and much beloved in the Mediterranean countries, has not been very much understood here except by those who enjoy Mediterranean cooking. Happily, people are learning to cook it in many more ways. Denuded of its beautiful dark and gleaming skin, it can look a little pathetic, but in this soufflé it doesn't. It's a delicate gray green in color almost like the Oriental celadon green and has an equally delicate flavor.

1 large eggplant, about 2 lbs., peeled and cut in chunks
2 tablespoons butter
⅓ cup finely chopped scallions with their green tops
2 tablespoons finely chopped sweet red bell pepper
3 eggs, separated
2 tablespoons fresh lemon juice
1 tablespoon finely chopped fresh dill or 1 teaspoon dried dill
salt

Put the chunks of eggplant in 2 quarts of boiling salted water and cook for 5 to 10 minutes until tender. Drain and mash, or blend until smooth and then press out some of the extra moisture in a sieve. (Don't push the eggplant through.) Mix gently with the scallions and pepper, egg yolks, lemon juice, dill, and salt. Whip the egg whites until they hold soft peaks and fold gently into the eggplant mixture. Turn into a 1-quart buttered and floured soufflé dish. Bake in a preheated 350° oven for 40 to 50 minutes. Serves 4.

Serve with broiled swordfish steak; leaf lettuce with cream dressing*; glazed oranges.

৺ BLACK BEAN SOUFFLÉ

A light and delicate version of an ordinarily robust bean.

1½ cups cooked dried black beans
(either soaked and simmered dried black beans or
the canned ones found in Spanish sections in markets, drained)
1 tablespoon grated orange rind
1 teaspoon dried mint
salt, if needed
5 egg whites, stiffly beaten
1 cup sour cream
2 tablespoons mandarin or curaçao liqueur

Purée the black beans and mix with the grated orange rind, mint, and a little salt if you like. (I like it without salt.) Put one spoonful of the beaten egg whites into the black bean purée and stir well. Fold the rest of the egg whites in gently. Turn into a buttered 5-cup soufflé dish and bake in a preheated 350° oven for 35 to 45 minutes. Serve immediately with a sauce of sour cream thinned with the mandarin or curaçao liqueur. Serves 4.

Serve with parsleyed ham*; raw mushroom salad*; frozen Alexanders*.

A Pleasure of Fungi

In ancient Egypt the pharaohs believed that mushrooms, which appeared so mysteriously overnight, were a divine and magical food. The Greeks, who learned about this wondrous food from them, called it the food of the gods, and so the wild ones still seem to be to those of us who seek them.

Now, instead of the capricious gods and the sometimes capricious effects of wild mushrooms, there are busy scientific people, mostly in a small part of Pennsylvania, who with *their* magic give us handsome, plentiful, always safe, and ever-delicious mushrooms that are available in most places the year around for a reasonable sum.

Mushrooms give a touch of elegance to everything they are cooked or served with, and yet they are distinguished by a delectable and enticing flavor when served alone in a very simple manner. They are always enhanced by butter and varying combinations of cream, lemon, wine, cheese, garlic, and onion, but these merely enhance the flavor of the mushrooms themselves rather than stand out on their own or take the upper hand.

Mushrooms have practically no calories and very little nutritional value, but according to the composer John Cage, founder of the New York Mycological Society, which is dedicated to the pursuit of the wild mushrooms, they make you feel so good that they increase your ability to digest other foods.

For the true mycophile, or mushroom lover, buying the convenient and safe mushrooms in our supermarkets never quite equals the adventure and delight of seeking and finding the wild ones. This can be as adventurous (and dangerous) as going on safari in Africa and much less costly. It may be done at odd moments in odd places. Old cemeteries are good hunting grounds (better than more recent ones); farms, our vanishing woods, orchards, and so on may have plentiful patches. Mycophiles, from the Greek word for fungus (mýkēs), are a widely varied, happy, dedicated, and compulsive group. But those who plan to eat mushrooms—the mycophagists (as differentiated from the scientific ones who merely want to collect and identify them)—are never unwary. Like many other foods, varying species and amounts of mushrooms will affect people in varying ways. The mushroom may be safe, but the eater may have a personal idiosyncrasy about it, as some do to chocolate, shellfish, or tomatoes. One mushroom, innocent in itself, will affect those who eat it only after they have had one or two cocktails; like antabuse, it makes one very sick.

Anyone considering this fascinating and dangerous sport is referred to Alexander H. Smith's book, *The Mushroom Hunter's Field Guide*, which is more explicit than most about these dangers. Once they are accepted and known, enjoy, enjoy. You will be one with Tolstoy, who returned from his first time out after a serious illness to which doctors and all Russia had given him up, shaky in the legs, somewhat sunburned, and proudly bearing a hatful of wild mushrooms he had picked. You will be one with Horace, the Roman poet and essayist, who said that the mushrooms that grow in the meadows have the sweetest flavor.

Most recipes for dishes that include mushrooms give flexible amounts, but cooking times are stricter. Except in stews, soups, and such, mushrooms—except for some wild varieties—should never be cooked more than ten minutes. Experts do not agree on whether mushrooms are to be washed or not, but all are against soaking in water. If mushrooms are washed, it should be under cold, running water, and they should be thoroughly dried with a towel. Mushrooms have so much moisture that any extra is unnecessary. Unless the mushrooms are old and tough, they should not be peeled. Fluting or carving mushroom caps is decorative and takes a certain amount of skill, but mushrooms are usually sliced, quartered through the cap and stem, or chopped fine. When chopped, the stems can be used for stuffing the caps or as additions to soups and other dishes.

One pound fresh mushrooms equals 1 quart whole mushrooms, 20 to 24 medium, 5 cups sliced, 4 cups minced or chopped, 3 cups duxelles*, or 3 ounces dried mushrooms.

❧ MARINATED RAW MUSHROOMS

These may be made from edible wild mushrooms or the white cultivated ones available in food stores.

½ cup olive oil
2 scallions, chopped (optional)
3 tablespoons tarragon vinegar or lemon juice
½ teaspoon salt
freshly ground black pepper
1 teaspoon pickling spice
½ lb. fresh mushrooms, sliced (or whole, if small)

Mix the oil, scallions, vinegar or lemon juice, and the seasonings together, crushing the seasonings with the back of a spoon or with a pestle. Add the mushrooms. Stir and toss well until all pieces are well coated. Let stand at room temperature for at least 3 hours. Makes about 3 cups.

Serve with party rye bread or slices of French bread, or plain with picks for grateful calorie watchers.

❧ RAW MUSHROOM SALAD

This is one of the best ways of serving mushrooms. Even mushrooms from the supermarket taste fresh from the earth.

½ lb. firm white mushrooms, cleaned
3 tablespoons olive oil
1 tablespoon lemon juice
1 infinitesimally small piece of garlic
salt, freshly ground black pepper
watercress (nice but not obligatory)

Cut the mushrooms lengthwise through the stem and cap into thin slices. Arrange them in a shallow glass or dark pottery plate.

Mix the olive oil, lemon juice, bit of garlic, salt, and pepper together, stirring slightly with a fork. Pour over the mushrooms. This salad must be done at the last minute, for the mushrooms will change color somewhat unattractively if dressed ahead of time. Serves 4— more if watercress is included. The watercress, if used, serves as a bed for the mushrooms.

Serve with Hungarian chicken*; parched rice with dried cherries*; lemon soufflé*.

◄§ MUSHROOM QUICHE

This quiche, richly studded with fresh mushrooms and heavy with their earthy aroma, makes a festive dish for Sunday breakfast, lunch, or a late supper.

2 teaspoons minced shallots
¼ cup butter
1 lb. fresh mushrooms, quartered
1 teaspoon salt
juice of ½ lemon
2 tablespoons sherry or Madeira
3 eggs
1½ cups heavy cream
pinch of nutmeg
1 8- or 9 inch partly baked pie shell (5 minutes)
⅓ cup freshly grated Swiss cheese

Preheat the oven to 375°. Sauté the shallots in a large skillet in 3 tablespoons of the butter over medium heat for about 1 minute. Add the mushrooms, salt, lemon juice, and wine. Cover and cook for 5 minutes, then uncover and cook, stirring, until the liquid has disappeared. Beat the eggs with the cream until they are barely mixed. Add the nutmeg. Spoon the mushroom mixture over the bottom of the pie shell. Pour in the egg and cream mixture. Sprinkle the top with the cheese and dot with the remaining butter.   Bake until set and lightly browned.   Serves 4 to 6.

Serve with Canadian bacon in one piece, roasted briefly; grapefruit Alaska*; champagne or a chilled white wine.

⋖ RISOTTO DI FUNGHI (MUSHROOM RISOTTO)

One of the most felicitous of vegetable dishes, with rice and mushrooms at their mutually enhancing best.   Fresh mushrooms or dried European mushrooms are good in this dish, but one really does need the short, stubby Italian rice called arborio, usually packaged in 1-pound cloth sacks.   It absorbs the butter much better than the regular long-grain Carolina rice.

¼ cup finely chopped onions
¼ lb. fresh mushrooms, sliced,
or 1 oz. dried mushrooms, soaked in water
4 tablespoons butter
1½ cups rice, preferably the Italian arborio
¾ cup dry white wine
2 cups (about) hot, good chicken broth
3 or 4 threads of saffron, pounded
more butter
freshly grated Parmesan cheese

Cook the onions and fresh mushrooms in the butter for 2 to 3 minutes.   (If dried ones are used, add with their soaking liquid *after* the rice and wine have been cooked together but *before* adding the chicken broth).   Add the rice to the onion and mushroom mixture and stir with a wood fork until the rice is permeated with butter.   Add the wine and cook over low heat until the wine is almost evaporated. (At this time add the dried mushrooms and their liquid if you are using them.)
Steep the saffron in the hot chicken broth while the wine is cook-

ing. The saffron is used partly for its elusive seasoning but partly for the beautiful color it gives to the rice. If for any reason there is none at hand, the color may be approximated, without impairing the quality of the dish, by cautiously adding powdered turmeric or 2 to 3 drops of yellow food coloring. Add the hot chicken broth to the rice a little at a time, keeping the dish simmering over very low heat. When the liquid has been absorbed and the rice is creamy, stir in 2 tablespoons each of butter and grated Parmesan cheese. Serve as soon as the cheese is melted. If this isn't possible, keep in a warming oven at low heat, and then serve with additional butter and cheese on separate plates. Serves 4.

Serve with watercress and arugula salad with vinaigrette made with lemon juice; strawberry and raspberry granita*; crisp chocolate cookies*.

◄§ TAGLIATELLI WITH HAM AND MUSHROOMS

The noodles do not need to be green, but I think they are prettier.

½ lb. tagliatelli or green noodles
½ lb. fresh or frozen mushrooms,
sliced and sautéed as an embellishment
6 thin slices prosciutto or baked Virginia ham,
cut in 2 x ½-inch strips
½ cup heavy cream
⅓ cup freshly grated Parmesan cheese
coarse breadcrumbs
butter
salt, pepper, if necessary

Cook the noodles in 2 quarts of boiling salted water until they are barely tender. Drain and put half the noodles into a medium, buttered casserole. Strew with half the mushrooms and half the ham. Make a second layer of noodles, mushrooms, and ham. Pour in the cream, sprinkle with the cheese and breadcrumbs, and dot with butter. If necessary, season with salt and pepper, but remember that the noodles have been seasoned while cooking, and that both the ham and cheese are salty. Bake in a preheated 350° oven for 35 minutes. Serves 4.

Serve with broiled tomato halves; lemon granita*; macaroons*.

༃ BEEF STROGANOFF

Most people whatever their taste are comfortable with this dish. Some Russians say that neither the mushrooms nor the tomato paste is found in the traditional version, but they are good American additions.

salt, pepper
2 lbs. beef tenderloin or boneless sirloin,
cut in 2 x ½ x ½-inch strips
½ cup butter
½ cup chopped onions
½ lb. fresh mushrooms, sliced thin
2 cups beef stock
1 teaspoon prepared mustard, preferably French Dijon type
1 tablespoon tomato paste
1 tablespoon flour
1 cup sour cream

Salt and pepper the meat and brown quickly in a skillet in half the butter. Remove with a slotted spoon to a plate. Add the onions to the pan and cook over a medium heat until they become translucent. Add the rest of the butter and the mushrooms. Cook for 5 to 6 minutes. Add the stock and cook for about 5 minutes. Add the meat and simmer until barely tender, about 5 to 10 minutes, stirring constantly. Mix the mustard, tomato paste, flour, and sour cream with a little of the juices from the pan. Add to the meat and mushroom mixture and cook just enough to heat thoroughly. Do not boil. Serves 6.

Serve with broccoli vinaigrette*, kasha*; coffee granita*.

≈§ CREAMED MUSHROOMS

As a sauce or a side dish, this is far preferable to the ubiquitous gummy white sauce with mushrooms.

3 tablespoons butter
1 clove garlic
¼ cup minced onions
1½ lbs. mushrooms, quartered
1 cup light cream
salt, pepper

Melt the butter in a skillet and heat the clove of garlic, removing it just before it browns. Add the onions and cook briefly; then add the mushrooms. Cook for about 5 minutes and add the cream, salt, and pepper, stirring until it thickens slightly. Makes about 2 cups.

Serve with baked meat loaf.

≈§ DUXELLES

A culinary blessing, this dish was first described by La Varenne, renowned seventeenth-century French chef and author of several cookbooks. It is a dry, but not dried, mushroom mixture that is instant magic for sauces, soups, soufflés, stuffing, and so on. It will keep in the refrigerator for several weeks and may be frozen. Stems may be used, or carefully identified wild mushrooms. One-half pound of finely chopped mushrooms measures 2 cups.

½ lb. cultivated mushrooms (whole or just the stems)
or wild mushrooms
2 tablespoons minced shallots or scallions
2 tablespoons butter
1 tablespoon oil
salt, pepper
¼ cup Madeira (nice but not obligatory)

Finely chop the mushrooms. Put them a few at a time into a towel and squeeze tightly, letting the juice run into a bowl. (It may be used later in a sauce or as a cooking essence or flavoring.) In a 8- or 9-inch skillet, sauté the mushrooms and shallots or scallions in butter and oil over fairly high heat so that any remaining moisture is evaporated by the time the mushrooms have cooked 6 to 7 minutes. Add salt and pepper. If the Madeira is used, add it now and cook until it too evaporates. Makes about 1½ cups duxelles.

A Benison of Ices and Creams

One of the most memorable moments of my early life was a summer night when I was permitted to stay up beyond my usual bedtime. Nick, an Italian ice-cream man, had stopped his horse and wagon by the entrance to my grandmother's across the street and rung his bell. Holding me by one hand, my father walked over to Nick. In his other hand my father carried an oval china vegetable dish that Nick filled generously with his homemade vanilla ice cream. I was so excited that my feet barely touched the ground.

Since then ice cream has been my treat and tranquilizer for all occasions, as it has been for many members of my family. One of my aunts, who lives in Pennsylvania near the New York border, was startled to be given a chest of community-plate silver by her local ice-cream store because she and her family had consumed in that year more ice cream than any other family in the county.

New Yorkers are always a little annoyed when they hear exaggerated stories about the wild lives they are reputed to live, but it was so even during George Washington's first term as President. Abigail Adams wrote to her sister in Boston to quell rumors that had been told there about the riotous life the Washingtons were living in New York. She said that the Washingtons entertained at a "Levey" or reception every "fryday at eight o'clock," and insisted that the company was entertained with "ice creems and Lemonade."

Although I too enjoy entertaining with ice cream, I also have it whenever I want it for myself, which is often. I frequently make granitas or sherbets in the freezing unit of my refrigerator, because these are easy to concoct and far better and less expensive than the bought ones. To make what are called snowballs, I scoop out balls of vanilla ice cream with a tablespoon, then roll them in shredded coco-

103

nut, which now and then I toast first. The shaggy balls are then well sprinkled with grated bitter chocolate, wrapped separately in foil, and put in the freezing unit until dessert time. Easy, elegant, and entertaining as well.

✑ BOMBE GLACÉE

A ceremonious and sophisticated way of serving ice cream is to fill a mold with two or more compatible flavors, sometimes with some small fruits or nuts between the layers.

First choose a simple mold that will hold the amount of ice cream you want to serve. Let the ice cream soften slightly. Line the mold with the variety you wish to have on the outside, such as the darkest color or the firmest. Put in the freezer until it hardens and then add nuts or fruits, pressing them against the hard lining. Fill the center with ice cream, sherbet, or whipped cream and freeze until hard. If the mold does not have a cover, fit aluminum foil around the top.

Some very handsome European ice-cream molds for bombes are designed with blow holes, so that one can free the bombe from the mold after arranging it on the serving plate by blowing through the holes. But any plain, unlined mold may be used and unmolded in the usual way: Loosen the ice cream by inserting a knife and running it around the edge. Then put the serving plate on top and upend the mold onto the plate. Drape a hot wet towel over the mold for a minute, just enough for the ice cream to slip out but not enough to melt it.

After unmolding, the bombe may be wreathed with flowers or small leaves or you may cover it with whipped cream and decorate it with crystallized roses, mint leaves, violets, or mimosa.

Some of the combinations that I particularly like are:

Black raspberry ice cream outside, raspberry sherbet in the center
Coffee ice cream outside, Russian pistachio ice cream*
in the center
Chocolate ice cream outside, with chopped hazelnuts pressed in
and coffee ice cream in the center

*Dark chocolate ice cream outside, with a center of whipped cream
and crystallized ginger mixed
Vanilla ice cream outside, with coarsely broken peanut brittle
pressed in, and apricot sherbet in the center*

Use the best-quality commercial ice cream or sherbet you can find
or make your own or use a combination of both.

Serve after carbonnade; spaetzle*; raw mushroom salad* with water-
cress.*

~§ COFFEE GRANITA

The Italians so far have left unsullied by progress their exquisite
grainy ices, or granitas, that are such a delight and such a contrast
to commercial ices or sherbets. This dessert is made of sweetened
diluted espresso coffee frozen to a grainy stage and served with heavy
cream, which is sometimes slightly whipped. There is nothing I
know of more cooling on a very hot day.

*1 cup espresso coffee
⅓ cup sugar
5 cups boiling water
1 cup heavy cream*

Put the coffee and the sugar in the filter-paper top of a large Melitta,
Chemex, or similar filter pot. Pour the boiling water, a little at a
time, over the coffee until it has all filtered through. Pour the coffee
into refrigerator trays or a metal mold and let it cool slightly before
putting into freezing unit. Leave the coffee about 45 minutes in the
freezer, then remove and put it in a bowl, scraping the frozen parts
from the sides and bottoms of the trays, and beat with an electric
beater. (If you prefer, simply whip the coffee with a spoon or wire
whisk until it is more or less mixed.) Return to the freezer for another hour or so. Remove once more and repeat the beating.

The granita should not be smooth. Freezing time will depend on your freezer or freezing unit, but the whole process usually takes 3 hours or so. You may let it stay in the freezer after the last beating and thaw it slightly before serving. I have occasionally deviated from the traditional technique and stirred in 3 unbeaten egg whites before freezing to slow the freezing process. Serve the granita piled in a glass bowl or goblet and top with the heavy cream, whipped or not as you like. Serves 4 to 6.

Serve after lamb with rice and apricots*; orange and black-olive salad*.

✒ LEMON GRANITA

Fresh and simple and lovely on a hot day, or at any time for that matter.

1 cup sugar

2½ cups water

1¼ cups fresh lemon juice

1 teaspoon grated lemon rind

3 egg whites (not traditional but prolongs keeping time)

Boil the sugar and water together for two or three minutes. Let cool. Add the lemon juice and lemon rind and, if you wish, 3 egg whites. (See directions about adding egg whites in the preceding recipe.) Stir well and pour into freezer trays or a mold and put in the freezer. After about 45 minutes, scrape the frozen parts and sides into the middle, which helps to make the mixture freeze more evenly. Return to the freezer. Do this once again after 45 minutes. Check before serving and if necessary remove from the freezer ahead of time. It should be mushy, rather like the consistency of fresh snow. Serves 4 to 6.

Serve after carbonnade*; spaetzle*; raw mushroom salad*.

❧ STRAWBERRY AND RASPBERRY GRANITA

This is a frozen version of the delectable Danish dessert often made with raspberries and currants and called rødfløde.

1 package frozen strawberries
1 package frozen raspberries
½ cup powdered sugar
¼ cup kirsch
juice of ½ lemon
3 egg whites

Put all ingredients in the blender and whirl until well mixed. Pour into freezing trays or a mold. After a half hour stir the frozen parts around the sides into the middle. Do it again once or twice This type of sherbet should be frozen to a mush, not into ice. Serves 4 to 6.

❧ COFFEE TORTONI

A heavenly mixture.

3 egg whites
3 tablespoons instant espresso coffee
pinch of salt
⅓ cup sugar and ¾ cup sugar, measured separately
3 cups heavy cream
½ teaspoon almond extract
2 tablespoons brandy or rum
1 cup slivered, browned almonds

Put the egg whites, coffee, and salt in a bowl and beat until stiff but not dry. Add ⅓ cup of the sugar bit by bit, beating after each addition until the mixture is stiff and satiny. Whip the cream separately, and after it is stiff, add the rest of the sugar, the almond extract, and the brandy or rum. Continue beating until blended, and fold with the nuts into the egg-white mixture. Pour into 12 paper dessert cups and put in the freezer. It becomes soft more quickly than ice cream does, so do not remove the cups from the freezer until about 10 to 15 minutes before serving. Also, do not make the dessert too far ahead of time, because it absorbs freezer odors. Serves 12.

Serve after Hungarian chicken*; risi-bisi (the rice pilaf with 1 cup cooked green peas); tossed green salad; French bread served hot with herb butter.

᪤ ORANGE-PEEL ICE

When my sisters and brother and I were young, we often had what we thought was the best of all orange ices. It was a pale, clear, orange-yellow ice with an almost bitter sharpness. We mourned its passing and have disdained the lurid colored and characterless ones on the market. Recently when making the glaze for glazed oranges, I realized that the tang of our childhood ice was in the syrup cooked with the peel. I made and strained the syrup, added orange juice, and froze it to a mushy consistency, and this is it. It will not please those who are accustomed to the bland versions. Once I left the slivered peel in the ice. It is delicate and pretty to look at, rather like Goldwasser liqueur when slightly shaken.

peel from 2 oranges
1 cup sugar
2 cups fresh orange juice

With a swivel vegetable knife, peel the skin thinly from the oranges, being careful not to get any of the bitter white. Cut the peel into tiny julienne strips about 1 inch long. Put in 1 cup cold water and heat, boiling for 2 to 3 minutes. Drain and reserve the peel. Put it into a small saucepan with sugar and 1 cup of fresh water. Bring to a boil, turn heat down to a simmer, and cook until thickened, or until a little syrup forms a soft ball when dropped into cold water. (On a sugar or fat thermometer the temperature will be 234° to 238° F.) Remove from the heat and let it cool. Add 2 cups orange juice. Freeze in ice-cube trays or charlotte mold. After 1 hour remove from freezing unit, stir well, and return to freezing unit. Freeze until mushy before serving. If it is more convenient to do this ahead of time and the ice becomes too hard, remove from the freezer and let stand at room temperature for about 20 minutes. Makes about 3½ cups.

Serve after picadillo with rice and beans; raw mushroom salad**
with watercress.

⋙ WATERMELON SHERBET

Sometimes, momentarily forgetful of all other beautiful fruits and vegetables, I think there is not one as lovely as a watermelon with its frosty delicate color. But it is a picnic fruit—not a party one—unless translated into a sherbet to be served ceremonially, perhaps in tulip champagne glasses or in a ring mold on a translucent platter, the center piled with black Bing cherries or (if one is lucky and the time is right) fresh blackberries. Surround the mold with freshly washed geranium or mint leaves.

1 envelope unflavored gelatin
2 tablespoons lemon juice
½ cup boiling water
¾ cup sugar
4 cups diced ice-cold watermelon (about ¼ medium-sized melon)
2 or 3 drops red vegetable coloring, 1 drop yellow
2 unbeaten egg whites

Put the gelatin, lemon juice, and boiling water in the blender. Cover and blend about 45 seconds. Remove the cover, add the sugar and 1 cup of watermelon cubes. Blend 15 seconds, remove cover, add 1 more cup of cubes. Cover and blend 15 seconds more.

Pour into a bowl. Blend the other 2 cups of watermelon cubes with the vegetable coloring and the 2 unbeaten egg whites for 30 seconds. Add to the mixture in the bowl and stir until well mixed. Pour into a metal mold or into several ice trays. Freeze for several hours, then remove, turn into a bowl, and beat well. Cover and return to the freezer until frozen. Serves 4 to 6.

Serve after broiled thick lamb chops; kugula*; watercress salad, sliced raw mushrooms, olive-oil and lemon-juice dressing with salt and freshly ground pepper; French bread and sweet butter; and with oak leaves*.

⊷§ WINE SHERBET

A sherbet often served as a nondessert or palate freshener with or after the meal. It is also a delight to those who prefer almost no dessert at all.

1 cup sugar
1 cup water
1 teaspoon grated orange rind
1 teaspoon grated lemon rind
½ cup orange juice (about 1 orange)
¼ cup lemon juice (more than 1 lemon)
4 cups dry white wine
2 envelopes unflavored gelatin
3 egg whites

Boil the sugar and water together for 5 minutes. Let cool. Add the rind and juice and all the wine except 1¼ cups. Soak the gelatin in ¼ cup of wine. Heat the remaining cup of wine, add the softened gelatin, and stir until dissolved. Add it to the juice and wine mixture and freeze until mushy. Remove, beat with wooden spoon or electric beater or put into blender. Beat the egg whites until stiff and fold them in. Return to freezer and freeze until firm, stirring once or twice. Transfer from freezer to refrigerator about ½ hour before serving. Makes 1½ quarts.

Serve after roast pork tenderloin; sweet potatoes flambé; chicory salad with vinaigrette dressing; coeur à la crème with whole fresh strawberries and unsalted crackers.

◆§ RUSSIAN PISTACHIO ICE CREAM

People I know who have been to Russia tell me that the food that delights and impresses them the most is the ice cream. There are three grades of Russian ice cream and what the travelers get is the top grade, called plombières. This is a French type with eggs and heavy cream, which is good in any country but not always easy to come by these days. It can be made in the freezing unit of a refrigerator, although of course it is always best made in larger amounts in a traditional ice-cream freezer. The pistachio recipe flavored with vanilla given here is more delicate than the kind we are used to. It's rather startling to realize that what we think of as pistachio ice cream is mostly green coloring and almond flavoring. Reality is much more subtle.

3 egg yolks
½ cup sugar
1 teaspoon real vanilla extract
3 cups heavy cream
a few drops green coloring (if you must)
1 cup (¼ lb.) shelled, unsalted pistachio nuts

Beat the eggs, sugar, and vanilla together until lemon colored. Then stir into the cream and cook very slowly over a low heat, stirring constantly until slightly thickened. Do not let the mixture get too hot or it will curdle. Add the green coloring very cautiously, unless you prefer to leave it out as I do. Strain the mixture through a sieve into ice-cube trays. Mix in the shelled nuts and freeze. Remove when it starts to get frozen around the edges. Beat and return to the freezer. Do this once or twice more. About 20 minutes before serving remove from the freezer. Serves 4 to 6 generously.

ᄤᅌ CRÈME FRAÎCHE

During my first trip to Paris in 1949 many foods were scarce or forbidden, among them crème fraîche. It was also the time when fraises des bois (wild strawberries) were in season, and I learned to love them served with the forbidden crème fraîche (happily, the French do not always take their laws too literally). Like many others I found the name confusing; it isn't of course fresh at all but a mature heavy cream. In New York these days it can be found but at a rather exorbitant price—more than five dollars a pint. In the meantime ingenious culinary Francophiles have devised several less costly ways of approximating the flavor.

Take 1 cup of heavy cream and put it in a screw-type jar with 1 tablespoon of buttermilk and shake it together for a minute or two. Allow it to stand at room temperature for 24 hours. Some people use a tablespoon of yogurt instead of buttermilk with the heavy cream, but this makes a very good sour cream, which is not the same thing. I'm told that in California, where almost anything can happen, an egg yolk is mixed with softened cream cheese, sour cream, and whipping cream. This is pleasant enough, but it isn't crème fraîche either. Makes 1 cup.

Serve with strawberries, raspberries, cherries, or blueberries.

ᄤᅌ SOUR-CREAM MOUSSE

A simple and beautiful dessert. Surround the mold with small fruits such as pitted black Bing cherries or raspberries. Despite the current uproar against any but fresh fruits (which too often aren't), the cherries may be canned or the raspberries frozen.

1 *quart sour cream*
1 *cup sugar*
½ *cup Cointreau, curaçao, or Grand Marnier*
1 *cup black Bing cherries or raspberries*

Mix all ingredients together and freeze. This may be done in a charlotte mold or a ring mold in the freezer. Remove from the freezer about 15 minutes before serving. This mousse doesn't really get hard and it melts very quickly. Serves 4.

Serve after Hungarian chicken*; Persian mäst*.

A Flattery of Innards

There is a whole new culinary field waiting for those adventurous enough to explore the many ways of cooking the insides and extremities of our edible animals and birds. It is my personal belief that we do not waste them but put them in hot dogs or pet food, depriving ourselves foolishly of these delicacies.

My first editor and I used to toss around the idea of a cookbook on this subject, to be called jokingly *The Awful Offal Cookbook*, using the forthright English name in preference to our euphemistic and colorless variety meats.

They continue to intrigue me and so I continue to read and cook. Once I even made Bath chaps, which is what the English call our hog jowls, but they were too fatty. I'm curious about chicken combs, which I have seen on a menu but did not eat, and chicken kidneys, which I've never seen. A Chilean man once described his favorite dish, cow udder with green sauce. What do we do with our cow udders? Hot dogs again, most likely.

Jane Grigson suggests in her excellent book *Good Things* that one of the reasons for the prestige and popularity of sweetbreads is their charming name. Perhaps if we called them thymus glands, which they are, we would react against them, as we do with kidneys, hearts, brains, tails, and tongues. "That which we call a rose by any other name would smell as sweet" does not, I think, apply to foods.

ঙ§ BEEF MARROW ON TOAST

A meltingly lovely and, in these days, uncommon and inexpensive treat. Marrow bones are not difficult to come by but cannot usually be found in the meat bins at the supermarket, though metropolitan markets sometimes have them marked "osso buco." Beef or veal bones, sawed in 2-inch pieces, can often be had on request, however.

Poach the bones in a little broth for 3 to 5 minutes or bake them *briefly* in a 350° oven, just enough to melt the marrow. Remove the marrow with a small demitasse spoon or a skewer; elegant and old-fashioned households use special marrow spoons. Spread on freshly made thin toast. Serves 2 as an appetizer.

ঙ§ PRESSED GIBLET LOAF

Once while meditating sorrowfully in front of the meat and poultry bins with their appallingly inflated prices, I came up with the idea for this dish. It is, one might say, a chicken headcheese, but whatever you call it, it's a good hot-weather dish, as good as it is cheap.

> 1 lb. chicken gizzards, or half gizzards and hearts
> 1 medium onion, chopped
> 1 bay leaf
> ½ teaspoon mixed pickling spice
> 1 envelope unflavored gelatin
> 2 tablespoons fresh lemon juice
> 1 tablespoon capers, drained
> 1 4-oz. can whole pimientos,
> drained and cut in ½-inch squares
> ⅓ cup finely chopped parsley

Put the giblets in a saucepan with the onion, bay leaf, pickling spice, and water to cover and simmer until tender. Remove the giblets and put them through a meat grinder, using the coarse disk. Strain the liquid (there should be about 2 cups broth—if not, add a little water). Soften the gelatin in the lemon juice with 2 table-spoons of fresh water. Heat the broth and the softened gelatin to-gether and stir until dissolved. Let cool slightly. Add the ground giblets, capers, pimientos, and finely chopped parsley. Put in a 8 x 5-inch loaf pan, press down firmly, and chill until firm. Serve sliced from the loaf pan. Serves 6 to 8.

Serve with spoon bread*; Bibb lettuce salad with cream dressing*; chocolate mousse*.

☙ DEVILED KIDNEYS

In English novels or Noel Coward plays, it always seems as if they were having deviled kidneys for breakfast. Somehow this dish re-minds us of a leisurely and secure life that is no more. And yet this is nonsense, for they are simple to prepare and not at all in the same economic class as caviar—far from it.

8 whole lamb kidneys
1 tablespoon prepared mustard
1½ teaspoons dry English mustard
2 tablespoons fresh lemon juice
pinch of salt
pinch of cayenne
2 tablespoons softened butter
4 slices of hot buttered toast

Slice the kidneys lengthwise, almost in half but not all the way through, and cut out the core of white fat in the center. Soak the kidneys in heavily salted cold water (2 tablespoons to the pint) to cover for about an hour to remove some of the flavor. After an hour drain and rinse the salt off. Mix the mustards, lemon juice, salt, and cayenne in a bowl and stir well. Add the kidneys and turn them about with a spoon. Let them stand at room temperature for an-other hour, stirring them from time to time. Take a baking pan that the kidneys will fit into in one layer and coat the pan with the softened butter. Preheat the broiler. Place the kidneys on the pan, cut side up. Broil 3 inches from the heat for 3 minutes, turn over, and broil 3 minutes more. Arrange 2 kidneys on each piece of toast and serve. Serves 4.

For Sunday breakfast, serve with scrambled eggs; sopaipilla; glazed oranges*; red wine.*

✑ SAUTÉED KIDNEYS IN FRENCH LOAVES

A sublime dish that makes your spirits soar.

> *1 long French loaf cut in 4 pieces*
> *1 tablespoons unsalted butter*
> *2 veal kidneys, cut in pieces, or 6–8 lamb kidneys*
> *¼ lb. sliced fresh mushrooms*
> *2 small cans Madeira sauce*
> *or 1¼ cups beef gravy with 2 tablespoons red wine*
> *1 tablespoon brandy*

Cut the pieces of bread lengthwise (but not all the way through), spread with some butter, and brown in the oven. Sauté the kidneys and the mushrooms in the rest of the butter for about 5 minutes. Add the Madeira sauce and the brandy. Put one toasted piece of bread on each plate and pour the kidney and mushroom mixture over it. Serves 4.

Serve with tomatoes and watercress.

✑ POLENTA RING
WITH CHICKEN-LIVER SAUCE

Polenta is the Italian version of our cornmeal mush, made with a finer ground meal not surprisingly called polenta meal. It is made traditionally in a huge copper pan and stirred with a wooden stick, usually by the man of the family. An Italian friend of mine remembers her father having a specially carved polenta stick. Polenta is served with many of the same sauces that are used on pasta. Sometimes it is used fresh from the pot with the sauce; other times it is poured onto a board or platter and allowed to cool. When cold and firm it is sliced about ½ inch thick, lightly floured, and then fried on both sides before serving. Many Italians prefer it that way.

1 quart of water
1 tablespoon salt
1 cup finely ground polenta meal (or white cornmeal)
⅔ cup peeled, seeded, and chopped tomatoes
4 tablespoons butter
1 teaspoon sugar
1 teaspoon salt
1 tablespoon cognac or brandy
1 lb. chicken livers, quartered
¼ cup dry white wine
¼ teaspoon sage

Bring the water and tablespoon of salt to boil in a large saucepan. Dribble the polenta meal slowly into the boiling water with your hand. Using a wooden spoon with a heavy handle, stir until medium thick. Pour into a greased ring mold holding slightly more than a quart and keep warm while you make the sauce. Sauté the tomatoes in 2 tablespoons of the butter. Add the sugar, salt, and cognac and simmer gently for a few minutes. Meanwhile sauté the chicken livers in another pan in the rest of the butter. Add the dry white wine and sage to the tomato sauce. Stir and then add the sautéed chicken livers. Let simmer on low heat while you unmold the polenta ring onto a large, dark platter. Pour the sauce over. Serves 4.

Serve with broccoli vinaigrette*; glazed oranges*.

⊸§ SURI LEBERLI (SWISS LIVER)

Calves' liver, as it was cooked and served at the old Swiss Pavillon in New York City, is delicate and ambrosial, quite a different dish from our robust way with fried onions and bacon, good as that is. Calves' liver is best cooked this way, but baby beef liver is very good too.

1½ lbs. calves' liver or baby beef liver
2 tablespoons butter
1 tablespoon finely chopped onion
1 jigger white wine, preferably Chablis
salt, pepper
1 teaspoon freshly chopped parsley

Pour boiling water over the meat and let it stand for 1 minute. Drain and cut the liver into thin strips about 2 inches long. Sauté the meat in half of the butter over high heat for about 2 minutes. Add the onion and sauté for another minute. Pour the wine over the meat. Light it with a match and let flame briefly. Add the remaining butter, sprinkle with salt, pepper, and parsley. Serve immediately. Serves 4.

Serve with green pasta with ricotta; peas in butter sauce; leaf lettuce salad with cooked carrots marinated in French dressing; sesame-seed rolls.

⊸§ CREAMED SWEETBREADS AND SCALLOPS

A creamy, sensuous party dish that requires only a brief cooking time and can be held in a double broiler. The preparation is not tedious, nor the time excessive.

2 pairs veal sweetbreads
1 tablespoon vinegar
1 lb. scallops, preferably small bay scallops

1 lb. fresh mushrooms, quartered
4 tablespoons butter
2 tablespoons flour
2 cups light cream
2 egg yolks, slightly beaten
salt, white pepper
¼ cup dry sherry
3 tablespoons finely chopped parsley
6–8 baked patty shells

Soak the sweetbreads in cold water for about an hour. Drain and put in a saucepan with cold water to cover and 1 tablespoon of vinegar. Bring to a boil and cook gently for 5 to 10 minutes. Drain and plunge the sweetbreads into ice water. When cool enough to handle, drain and skin them. Remove the connective tissue, drain on paper towels, and cut into large dice. Cut the bay scallops in half (sea scallops in quarters), add the sliced mushrooms, and sauté them very, very briefly in 2 tablespoons of the butter. Set aside.

Using the top of a double boiler (one large enough to hold the sweetbreads, scallops, and mushrooms), melt the remaining butter with the flour, stirring well for a few minutes. Add the cream, a little at a time, stirring until smooth and slightly thickened. Remove a tablespoon of the sauce and mix with the beaten egg yolks and add them to the sauce. Stir over low heat for a few minutes until somewhat thickened. Season with salt and white pepper to taste. Stir in the sherry and parsley, then add the sweetbreads, scallops, and mushrooms. Set the top of the double boiler over simmering water that does not reach the bottom of the top pan and keep until needed. Serve in warm patty shells. Serves 6 to 8.

Serve with Italian green bean salad*; champagne; strawberry and raspberry granita*; oak leaves*.

A Freshening of Lemons

Is there any fruit as lovely to look at as a fresh lemon, a fruit whose flavor in both juice and rind can add so much to so many dishes? Even a few drops subtly insinuated into a sauce or splashed onto steaks, fish, and vegetables or mixed into soups, cakes, and soufflés can make an enormous, rewarding difference between merely satis factory and eminently satisfying.

When one thinks of avgolemono, that delicate and sublime Greek soup, or veal piccata, perhaps the simplest and best of all veal dishes, lemon soufflé and mousse, Marlborough pie and lemon granita and so many other dishes in nearly every cuisine, it would seem fitting to pour a libation to the lemon—perhaps at the foot of a lemon tree.

According to Theophrastus, the Greek philosopher (around 300 B.C.) and author of the six-volume *Causes of Plants* (one of my favorite titles), citron, *Citrus medica,* the prototype of lemon (which even now exists in candied form for fruitcakes), was used in perfuming clothes and was probably the first and nicest of all mothballs.

The origin of the lemon, *Citrus limonia,* is uncertain, but the fruit is known to have appeared in Spain and North Africa between 1000 and 1200. The Crusaders found it in Palestine and took it to Europe. By 1494—two years after Columbus's first trip to America—it was being grown in the Azores and being shipped to England. Lemons are now grown in countries around the Mediterranean, although the largest percentage of the world crop comes from the United States. It is surprising that the lemon survived and flourished so well, for the lemon tree is more tender than the orange or grapefruit, easily injured by high temperatures as well as low ones. It must be grafted onto other citrus stock, usually orange, and ripened under carefully controlled conditions.

In buying lemons, select those that feel heavy and have a thin glistening skin with fine "pores." This is easier said than done, for most supermarket lemons have dry, dull, thick skins with relatively little juice. (If they are slightly green, don't worry.) Any lemon dropped in boiling water for two minutes and then cooled slightly before squeezing will yield more juice. For the zest—the lovely yellow rind—peel thinly with a swivel-bladed vegetable knife, avoiding the bitter white pith. Mince fine, or better yet, put the zest in an electric coffee grinder. It's an integral part of gremolata, and adds zing to salad dressings, simple syrup for tea, soufflés, butter, fish, hamburger, et cetera, et cetera.

✑ AVGOLEMONO SOUP (GREEK EGG-AND-LEMON SOUP)

One of the truly great and simple soups of the world.

8 cups strong clear homemade chicken broth
½ cup rice
4 eggs
juice of 2 lemons
parsley clusters

Bring the broth to a boil, add the rice, and cook over a low heat until the rice is tender, about 20 to 30 minutes. Turn the heat down. Beat the eggs with a whisk or rotary beater until light and foamy. Add the lemon juice and beat some more. Add 2 cups of the hot soup and beat until well mixed. (Or put the eggs and lemon juice in a blender, cover and blend for a minute, remove the top and slowly add the 2 cups of soup while the blender is going.) Add the diluted egg-and-lemon mixture to the rest of the soup, beating constantly. Heat almost to the boiling point but not quite or the soup will curdle. Serve it immediately, sprinkled with parsley clusters. Serves 6 to 8.

Serve before broiled salmon steaks with anchovy butter; creamed spinach; tiny boiled new potatoes; cherry turnovers.

✑ LEMON CHICKEN

The simple lemon-and-egg thickening used in Greek cookery—
the beginning of both mayonnaise dressing and hollandaise sauce—
appears in a still different guise in this dish.

flour
salt, pepper
1 2½-to-3-lb. chicken, cut up
2 tablespoons salad oil
2 eggs
juice of 1½ lemons
1 tablespoon grated lemon rind
1 cup warm chicken broth

Flour and season the chicken lightly. Sauté in oil until golden
brown on both sides. Place the chicken pieces in a shallow casserole.
Beat the eggs and add the lemon juice and grated rind. Beat some
more. Add the warm chicken broth slowly, beating after each addition. Pour the mixture over the chicken. Bake in a 350° oven for
25 to 30 minutes, or until chicken is tender. The lemon sauce,
which is almost a custard, is better if not cooked too long. Some
broth may settle at the bottom of the custard, but that is all right.
Serves 4.

Serve with asparagus; mixed green salad; butterflake rolls; ice cream.

✑ VEAL PICCATA

Although veal is not easily found in this country except in the
large cities, it is a very delicate meat and can be absolutely delicious
cooked in many ways. Very fine veal is very high priced, and it seems
odd nowadays that at one time people would stretch their chicken
with the lower-priced veal. Now even the Italians in our country
who take veal seriously are using chicken or turkey in many dishes
traditionally made of veal. To me veal cooked in the following
manner is at its most sublime. It needs no embellishment.

1 lb. veal cut into thin slices as for scaloppini
½ cup flour
salt, freshly ground black pepper
2 tablespoons sweet butter
¼ cup olive oil
2 tablespoons fresh lemon juice
1 lemon cut in very thin slices
finely chopped parsley

Even if you have the butcher pound the slices thin, you will have to pound them some more at home. Put them between two pieces of wax paper and pound with a mallet or the bottom of an empty wine bottle until *very* thin. Mix the flour and seasonings and dust the veal lightly on both sides. Heat the butter and oil in a skillet almost to the smoking stage. Then add the veal slices. Cook quickly over high heat on both sides until golden. Transfer to a warm platter. Heat the lemon juice briefly in the same skillet. Pour over the veal, garnish with lemon slices, and sprinkle with the chopped parsley. Serves 4.

Serve with spaetzle*; Italian green bean salad*; frozen preserved ginger in whipped cream*.

~§ CARROT PURÉE WITH LEMON JUICE

I don't often buy carrots or think much about cooking them, but I like them this way.

2 cups raw sliced carrots (about 1 lb.)
½ cup water
3 tablespoons melted butter
½ teaspoon sea salt or a bit more of table salt
freshly ground black pepper
2 tablespoons sugar
3 tablespoons lemon juice

Put all the ingredients in container of blender and blend until carrots are all ground. Pour into a heavy saucepan and cook over low heat for 30 minutes or more, stirring occasionally until liquid has evaporated and the raw taste has vanished. Serves 3 to 4.

Serve with broiled swordfish steak; Italian green bean salad*; espresso.

❧ LEMON BUTTER

This is a composed butter, as the French say, a softened butter mixed with seasonings and kept in the refrigerator or freezer on the ready. Put a spoonful or two on broiled steak, broiled tuna or salmon, or broiled chicken, or even on baked potato.

> *½ cup butter or margarine*
> *2 teaspoons grated lemon rind*
> *juice of ½ lemon*
> *1 teaspoon chopped garlic*
> *2 tablespoons chopped parsley*

Mix all ingredients and pack into a suitable jar. Keep covered in the refrigerator or freezer. Makes a little over ½ cup.

❧ LEMON-CURD TART FILLING

This is a much-loved, old-fashioned recipe usually thought to be English but turning up occasionally in books on other cuisines such as that of the Pennsylvania Dutch. It is sometimes called lemon butter, perhaps because it is used as a delectable spread for toast— or crumpets and other breakfast and tea breads—but it shouldn't be confused with the preceding recipe. Tarts filled with this mixture have been called lemon chess, although quite dissimilar from other Southern chess pies. The proportions also vary, especially the amount of sugar used, but the basic ingredients always remain unchanged. This can be bought in jars but it is much better and quite simple to make at home.

6 tablespoons unsalted butter (¾ of a stick)
¾ cup sugar
¾ cup fresh lemon juice (about 3 large lemons)
6 egg yolks
4 teaspoons grated lemon rind

Cook the butter, sugar, lemon juice, and egg yolks in a heavy-bottomed pan or the top of a double boiler, stirring with a wooden spoon until the spoon is well coated. Remove from the heat. Stir in the lemon rind and turn into a bowl or jar to cool. Keep in the refrigerator until needed as a spread or a filling for tarts. Makes about 1½ cups and keeps 2 weeks or more.

◄§ FRESH ORANGE AND LEMON DROP COOKIES

Old-fashioned lemon drop cookies in an easy tart version, which I think I like even better.

1 ½-inch slice orange
2 ¼-inch slices lemon
1 egg
¼ cup (1 stick) butter softened
1 cup sugar
1½ cups flour
¼ teaspoon baking soda

Seed and quarter the orange and lemon slices. Combine them with the egg, butter, and half the sugar in the blender and mix well. Turn into a bowl, add the rest of the sugar, flour, and soda. Drop by teaspoonsful 1 inch apart onto greased cookie sheets. Bake in a preheated 375° oven for 15 minutes. Makes 40 to 50 small cookies. This recipe may easily be doubled.

◄§ LEMON CAKE

I seldom make large, important layer cakes, but I do like to make small, unserious ones from time to time. This is a light and fresh-tasting cake that freezes well.

¾ stick unsalted butter, softened
½ cup sugar
2 eggs, slightly beaten
½ cup warm milk
1½ cups sifted all-purpose flour
1½ teaspoons baking powder
¼ teaspoon salt
1½ tablespoons grated lemon rind

TOPPING:
¼ cup fresh lemon juice
½ cup sugar

Cream the butter and sugar together, beating with a wooden spoon until fluffy. Add the slightly beaten eggs. Beat until mixed, then add the milk. Add the flour sifted with the baking powder and salt, a little at a time, and stir in the grated lemon rind. Beat well until smooth. Pour into a greased 9 x 9 x 2-inch pan and bake in pre-heated 350° oven for 25 minutes. Remove from the oven briefly. Mix the lemon juice and sugar and spoon over the hot cake. Bake 5 minutes more until the lemon juice is soaked in and the top is dry. This is good served slightly warm. Cut into 9 or 12 pieces. This recipe can be doubled if you're feeding a crowd.

Serve after Hungarian chicken*; risotto di funghi*; watercress salad.

◄§ MARLBOROUGH APPLE PIE

Even though in a small Pennsylvania town on the Susquehanna two of my ancestors' tombstones have incised on them "scalped by the Indians," I do not care to be described as being as American as apple pie. The traditional version is rather dull and uninteresting looking to me even at its best. But this Marlborough pie made with applesauce voluptuously enriched by eggs and butter and sharpened with lemon is golden and beautiful and exciting to eat. If the crust is baked in a straight-sided flan ring or cake tin, it is much more elegant looking than the kind with sloping sides.

1 cup tart applesauce
3 tablespoons lemon juice
1 teaspoon grated lemon rind
1 teaspoon cinnamon
½ cup sugar or more to taste
3 tablespoons melted butter
½ teaspoon salt
4 eggs
1 9-inch unbaked pie crust

Put all the ingredients except the pie crust in the container of the blender and buzz until well mixed. Pour into the unbaked pie shell. Put in an oven preheated to 400°. Bake 15 minutes, then reduce heat to 300°. Bake about 45 minutes more. The filling becomes firm as it cools. It may be served then or made ahead and chilled in the refrigerator. Serves 6.

Serve after parsleyed ham*; Armenian pilaf*; fennel and cucumber salad with oil-and-vinegar dressing.

◆§ LEMON MOUSSE

Sometimes called fromage, sometimes a cold soufflé, other times bavarois au citron, but whatever the name it's a fresh, lemony tasting, velvety, sensuous mixture of lemon juice and eggs and whipped cream, a perfect party dish that can be made ahead. It is visually enhanced when chilled and served in a clear dish such as a plain straight-sided glass soufflé baking dish.

1 tablespoon gelatin
¼ cup cold water
3 eggs, separated
1 cup sugar
juice and grated rind of 2 large lemons
2 cups heavy cream
1 tablespoon confectioners' sugar
1 teaspoon vanilla

Soften the gelatin in the cold water and dissolve *over* hot water, not in. Beat the egg yolks until thick and pale yellow. Stir in the sugar, lemon juice, and grated rind. Beat the egg whites until stiff but not dry and whip 1½ cups of the heavy cream. Fold the dissolved gelatin into the lemon mixture. Fold in the egg whites and then the whipped cream. Pour the mixture into a 1½-quart soufflé dish. It sets fast but should chill 2 to 3 hours at least. Whip the last ½ cup of cream with the confectioners' sugar, add the vanilla, and spread it on top of the mousse. Serves 6.

Serve after mutton ham (see recipe for flageolets à la crème); spaetzle** *with crumbs and butter; mixed green salad.*

৶ LEMON SOUFFLÉ WITH STRAWBERRIES

A light and lovely dessert, this may be prepared as much as an hour before you start to bake if a larger bowl is inverted over the soufflé dish.

2 tablespoons butter
2 tablespoons flour
½ cup sugar
⅓ cup heavy cream
⅓ cup lemon juice
2 tablespoons grated lemon rind
pinch of salt
5 eggs, separated
1 cup sugared, hulled fresh strawberries

Melt the butter in a heavy saucepan and add the flour, cooking and stirring until well blended and thickened slightly. Using a wooden spoon, stir in the sugar and cook for a minute or two; then add the heavy cream. Stir until smooth and thickened. Add the lemon juice, grated lemon rind, and salt. Stir until blended. Remove from the fire, let cool a minute or two, then stir in the egg yolks. Whip the whites until they make stiff peaks. Add a spoon of the lemon mixture to the egg whites and mix gently before folding the whites into the lemon mixture. Sprinkle the strawberries in the bottom of a small soufflé dish (about 2½ cups) that has been previously buttered and sprinkled with sugar. Bake in a preheated 350° oven for about 35 minutes. Serve immediately. Serves 2.

Serve after chicken breasts with tarragon*; capellini*; watercress and arugula salad with vinaigrette dressing.

A Gluttony of Nuts

To me nuts are a glorious addiction. Along with many Europeans, I think them a bewitching addition to almost any dish, transforming simple foods into culinary masterpieces as they increase food values in an unobtrusive manner. So I revel in dishes such as praline soufflé, cranberry nut bread, cold Turkish chicken with walnut sauce, capellini with walnuts and garlic, pistachio ice cream, macaroons, chicken salad with Brazil nuts, and so on. And all by themselves—roasted and in their shells—they remind me of Christmas stocking stuffers or that Victorian custom of cracking and eating walnuts while sipping after-dinner port.

Nuts are a sound, serious, and compact source of protein and include many other needed nutrients. They have what are called "armored" calories—those that are nourishing as well as fattening—so one can be both guilt-free and satisfied while eating them.

The nuts that I prefer for cooking and eating out of hand are almonds and hazelnuts (or filberts). I also use pignolias and walnuts frequently in cooking but seldom for eating otherwise. I have always wondered why I feel that way about walnuts. Is it that I don't like the muddled design? Pignolias, I know, are just too tiny. They are an Italian form of pine nut but may be used interchangeably with the southwestern American piñons, which are of a different species. Pignolias are always sold shelled and piñons (also known as Indian nuts) are always sold in the shell. Native-born New Mexicans put the nuts in their mouths and spit out the shells with a good deal of skill, but outlanders never seem to develop the knack.

Macadamias are beautiful and expensive—the nut equivalent of caviar or truffles, though rather more affordable.

It suits me best to buy nuts loose (shelled but otherwise untampered with) from health-food or specialty stores, although I have used vacuum canned ones in a pinch. (I always avoid buying those oversalted and stale nuts in small cellophane packages.)

ᵔᶳ SALTED ALMONDS

Surprisingly enough, one of the most pleasing of all appetizers is a dish of salted almonds prepared at home. It matters not whether they are served alone with the evening tipple or as part of an assortment of hors d'oeuvre. There is a shock of delight for everyone whose taste buds have been blunted by the uninspiring versions available commercially.

Start with shelled almonds, brown skins intact. Drop them briefly for one or two minutes in boiling water until the skins are loose and puckery looking. Drain in a colander and rinse with cold water. When cool enough to handle, pinch off the pointed tips and slip off the skins. Arrange on an oiled cookie sheet and put in a preheated 300° oven just until they are lightly browned. You may also do this in a large skillet on top of the stove. Remove them to a square of aluminum foil large enough to fold around the nuts. Drizzle one or two tablespoons of melted unsalted butter over the nuts and shake them around. Sprinkle generously with a coarse salt, either sea or kosher. Elizabeth David thinks that the nuts have a better flavor if the foil is folded lightly around them and they are allowed to sit for about two hours before serving. She suggests keeping them in a drawer during this time to protect them from premature pilfering.

ᵔᶳ BRAZIL-NUT CHIPS

An unstereotypical nibble for pre-dinner drinkers.

Brazil nuts are hard to shell—that is, unless you know the easy way. Cover the nuts with cold water, bring to a boil, and boil over medium heat for three minutes. Drain, plunge into cold water for a minute or two. Drain again and crack. The larger pieces of nut meat will come away from the shell easily. Slice the pieces thin lengthwise. Spread out in a shallow pan. Dot with butter and sprinkle with coarse salt, preferably sea salt. Bake in a preheated 350° oven for 15 to 20 minutes, stirring occasionally. These can also be used to garnish salads featuring meat, seafood, or poultry. If you plan to decorate cakes with them, omit the salt.

☙ WALNUT AND GARLIC SOUP

Absolute bliss, especially on a very hot day. It may be served hot or cold but I much prefer the latter.

1 cup shelled walnuts
1 plump garlic clove
4 cups boiling chicken broth
salt, freshly ground black pepper, if needed
½ cup heavy cream

Put the walnuts and the garlic in the blender and buzz until smooth. Add half the boiling chicken broth and blend until mixed. Pour into a soup tureen and stir in the rest of the chicken broth. Check the seasonings and add more if necessary. Let it cool before you stir in the heavy cream. Chill thoroughly before serving. Serves 4 to 6.

Serve before lamb shanks with dried fruit*; rice; watercress salad with vinaigrette dressing; chocolate mousse*.

☙ CAPELLINI

One anticlerical Italian-American family I knew always served this as part of a festive, fasting Christmas Eve meal that included broiled eel and stuffed escarole. I serve it with non-Italian dishes at any time of the year, because it appeals to both sophisticated palates and the unadventurous variety. It is easy to assemble once you have found capellini, the thinnest of all pasta. (The name means "fine hair.") The pasta takes about a minute to cook, more and it gets too squashy.

3 whole cloves garlic
salt, pepper
¼ cup olive oil
1 lb. capellini
½ cup coarsely chopped walnuts

Heat the garlic, salt, and pepper in the olive oil but do not brown. Cook the pasta in rapidly boiling salted water until it is barely tender (about a minute or so). Drain. Remove the garlic from the olive oil and discard. Pour the olive oil over the hot pasta and toss with a fork and spoon until each strand is coated with the seasoned olive oil. Sprinkle with the chopped walnuts. Serve immediately. Serves 4 generously.

Serve with lemon chicken*; Italian green bean salad*; chocolate mousse*.

⊷§ ESCAROLE WITH RAISINS AND PINE NUTS

This is a traditional Italian-American dish for the festive Christmas Eve meal, but I find it appropriate to serve anytime to untraditional Americans. It is a nice change from the usual green vegetables.

1 medium head of escarole
⅓ cup golden seedless raisins
⅓ cup pine nuts or pignolias
½ cup chicken broth

Wash the head of escarole under running water but do not separate the leaves. Shake as dry as possible and pat with paper towels to get rid of any residual moisture. Press the leaves open slightly and sprinkle the raisins and pignolias in among them as evenly as possible. Tie the leaves together loosely at the ends with a string. Bring the chicken broth to a boil and add the escarole. Cover and steam briefly over low heat, just enough to soften the escarole but not to wilt it completely. Untie the string, drain, and serve in a round bowl. Serves 4.

Serve with meat loaf with apricots*; lemon soufflé*.

⚜ CIRCASSIAN COLD CHICKEN

One of the most beautiful and most sophisticated of the cold chicken dishes is of Turkish origin, found now on the Mediterranean and elsewhere. Traditionally, the walnuts, almonds, or filberts are ground over and over again until an oil appears. This oil is mixed with the paprika and used to decorate the mound of chicken. In our short-cut culture, however, walnut oil, olive oil, or almond oil is used.

> *3 cups cut-up cooked chicken (see poached chicken*)*
> *2 cups chicken broth*
> *2 cups ground walnuts*
> *oil*
> *paprika*

Cut the cold cooked chicken in neat strips or dice and arrange it in a mold on a pretty glass platter. Mix the chicken broth and the walnuts into a paste and spread over the mound of chicken. Mix a little oil with the paprika and make a pleasing design on the mound. Picasso decorated one once for Gertrude Stein and Alice B. Toklas. Serves 6.

Serve with Armenian pilaf*; watercress; coffee granita*.

✥ YELLOW TOMATO, SCALLION, AND BLACK WALNUT SALAD

Admittedly yellow plum-shaped tomatoes are not a staple in every home and shop, but they are well worth growing or searching for. The flavor is delicate, the color lovely, and they are a pleasing change from the ubiquitous red. Black walnuts, too, are uncommon but they have a wonderful gamy flavor and are well worth the trouble of finding. I find their shells unopenable, so I buy them shelled and sometimes canned. Don't serve them to the unwary without a warning about the strange musky flavor. English walnuts are also good but not quite so exotic.

1 lb. yellow plum tomatoes
¼ cup chopped scallions with part of their green tops
2 tablespoons chopped black walnuts or English walnuts
vinaigrette dressing

Dip the yellow plum tomatoes, a few at a time, into boiling water for a minute or two, then remove and skin. Cool and halve. Mix with the scallions and walnuts. Add the vinaigrette. To show this dish at its best, serve in glass or wooden bowls. Serves 4.

Serve with lima beans baked in sour-cream sauce*; glazed oranges*.

✥ BEET AND ENDIVE SALAD WITH WALNUTS

A crisp and flavorful change from the usual salad standbys.

1 cup diced cooked beets
½ cup walnut halves
1 lb. fresh, firm Belgian endives, cut 1-inch long
4 tablespoons olive oil
1 tablespoon red wine vinegar
1 teaspoon French prepared mustard
salt, freshly ground black pepper

Mix the diced beets, walnuts, and endives in a salad bowl (black is beautiful for this combination). Stir together the olive oil, vinegar, mustard, and salt and pepper to taste. Spoon over the salad. Serves 4.

Serve with lemon chicken*; spaetzle* with buttered crumbs; chocolate mousse*.

◄§ MACAROONS

Since I don't have a well-developed sweet tooth, I am seldom moved to ecstasy by the sight of cakes and cookies, but homemade macaroons turn me on. Yet they are very simple to make, so delicate and lovely that it is surprising they aren't served more often. They are almost as easy to make as a ready-mix, though one must allow time for drying before baking. They may be made with ground almonds or an 8-oz. can of almond paste, but I prefer the ground nuts, which are easy enough thanks to the blender.

> *1½ cups blanched, finely ground almonds*
> *1 cup sugar*
> *2–3 egg whites*

Mix the almonds and sugar together and stir in the egg whites, one at a time, until you get a moist and firm consistency. This can vary quite a bit, but don't worry so long as the mixture is soft but not liquid. Let the mixture rest for several hours at room temperature. Then take a tablespoonful at a time, roll it into a ball, and flatten slightly. Each cookie should be about 1½ inches across and ½ inch thick. Put on a buttered baking sheet. Let the cookies dry again for about an hour. Bake them in a slow oven (325°) for 10 to 20 minutes. Do not let them brown. Remove and allow them to dry a little more before putting them in a cookie tin. Makes 2 dozen.

Serve after cold pork tenderloin with rosemary-scented apricot aspic*; spoon bread*; and with coffee granita*.

⋖§ PRALINE SOUFFLÉ

Any recipe for a sweet soufflé may be used with a half cup of praline powder added. This soufflé requires a somewhat different technique from the traditional type, one suggested by the late Albert Stockli.

1 cup milk
5 eggs, separated
4 tablespoons flour
3 tablespoons softened butter
1 teaspoon vanilla
½ cup praline powder (see the following recipe)

Heat but don't boil the milk in a medium-sized, heavy-bottom saucepan. Have the egg whites in one bowl and the egg yolks in another. Beat the yolks until lemon colored and sift the flour into the egg yolks, stirring until you achieve a smooth paste. Gradually add about half the hot milk along with all the softened butter and stir until smooth. Add this mixture to the remaining milk in the pan and cook over low heat, stirring constantly until the batter thickens. Remove from the heat, add the vanilla and praline powder to the mixture, and stir well. Beat the egg whites until they form soft peaks. Add a spoonful of the egg whites to the batter, mixing thoroughly, then fold the rest in gently. Pour the soufflé batter into a 1½- to 2-quart buttered and sugared soufflé dish. Bake in a preheated 450° oven for 15 minutes, then reduce the temperature to 400°. At this point the soufflé should have risen over the top of the dish. Insert a pointed knife straight down along one edge of the dish and cut all around. The soufflé will rise even higher and will not spill over the sides. Bake at 400° for another 15 minutes, or until the top is golden brown. Serve immediately. Serves 4 to 6.

Serve after Maryland stuffed ham; parched rice with dried cherries*;* *mixed green salad.*

ᥱ PRALINE POWDER

The crunchy texture of nuts has always appealed to me as much as their rich, oily taste, but until I first learned about praline powder, I hadn't realized how subtle and beguiling the flavor of nuts could be. It is a nut brittle made with sugar syrup which is ground into powder and used to enhance many desserts—a mousse, a soufflé, a filling for a cake or a torte, a Paris-Brest*, or a chocolate broyage*. Almonds or hazelnuts or a combination of the two are the nuts I like to use for this powder. Some people skin and toast the nuts, but others use them as they are after shelling. Both ways are good. One may also vary the proportions for the sugar syrup. The only thing that can really go wrong is burning the nuts, so keep a careful watch.

> *1 cup blanched almonds, or 1 cup filberts (hazelnuts),*
> *or a combination*
> *1 cup sugar*
> *¼ teaspoon cream of tartar*
> *¼ cup water*

Toast the nuts on a greased cookie sheet in a preheated 350° oven for 10 to 15 minutes. The filbert skins may be rubbed off between paper towels easily at this point. Combine the sugar, cream of tartar, and water and boil until golden in color. Then add the nuts, stir around, and pour onto a buttered cookie sheet or pan. When hard and cool, grind in the blender. This powder will be fine, but a coarser ground is sometimes good in a mousse or filling. Put in a screw-top jar and keep at room temperature. Makes 1½ cups.

ᥱ NUT PIE CRUST

Because I love nuts, it naturally follows that I should like a nut pie crust, an elegant version of a cracker or a cookie crust. It is good

filled with the chocolate mousse* or whipped cream with a half cup
of praline powder* stirred into it.

1½ cups Brazil nuts, walnuts, or hazelnuts, ground
3 tablespoons sugar
¼ cup melted butter

Mix the nuts, sugar, and butter together. Press the nuts to the
bottom and sides of an 8-inch pie tin with the back of a spoon.
Bake at 400° for about 15 minutes.

A Lift of Picnics

A picnic is much more than a shared meal eaten in the open—the dictionary definition. It is a state of mind, a mood, a free-spirited approach to living.

There are some sad people who never know this special delight, some who never know the peace of sharing tarragon chicken and good Bourbon in the clear air and uninhabited silence of a New Mexican mountain at sunset; the euphoria that comes from eating delicatessen sandwiches with gin-and-tonic on an abandoned fish wharf with the sun setting on the Chesapeake; or even the prosaic but positive pleasure of grilling hot dogs in your own backyard. There are the people who start muttering about ants when the picnic mood quickens in others. Let them be. Efforts to change their attitude are usually a waste of time.

The people who do like picnics are a happy and dedicated breed. Almost any pretext will do, a stray suggestion, a vagrant breeze, or a balmy day. Not even the time of year seems to discourage some picnickers. One friend of mine especially likes bird-watching picnics in winter, with home-cooked food served in a warm car and a pair of binoculars close at hand.

One of my favorite women, whom I know only from her lively letters written between 1709 and 1762, is Lady Mary Wortley Montagu. Most people like best the letters she wrote from Turkey when her husband was a diplomat there, but in my copy of the book, much battered by rereading, I take a special delight in her later years, when her life was in fact a picnic. She bought a semi-ruined palace at Louverre, in Venetia, Italy, but spent most of her time at a nearby dairy house with one big room. The floor was strewn with rushes, the chimney covered with moss and branches. She added some straw chairs, a couch, and some earthenware bowls full of flowers and set a table that would seat twenty in the garden among fruit trees, grape arbors, and tea bushes. Once she entertained Lord Rosebery for breakfast, giving him bread and butter of her own manufacture. She stayed happily on her more-or-less self-sustaining farm, reading boxes of books that were sent her from London, writing and receiving letters, and enjoying her wonderful picnics until the year before she died.

❧ TEA

In my earlier years I used to drink many pots of green tea with friends at a single sitting, tea brewed in the Chinese way, and drunk without sugar, cream, or lemon. We were able to solve many of the world's problems and to discover the true meaning of the books we were reading. Though my stimulant is now coffee, my favorite hot-weather drink continues to be iced tea, which I prefer even to fresh lemonade and fruit juices.

To make tea the Chinese way, pour the boiling water over green tea leaves in a heated pot, allowing one teaspoon of leaves for each cup with an extra teaspoon for the pot. Let it steep for four minutes and *no more.* Then pour the tea off into another hot china or pottery teapot and serve. This way the strong tannin flavor that I find objectionable has no chance to develop.

Iced tea should be made from a good black tea. It should be made with boiling water, in much stronger proportions than the hot, and then cooled. Or it may be made cold, a method that surfaces from time to time in print. Allowing 1 tablespoon of tea for each cup of cold water, put tea and water into a glass or pottery jug, and let it stand for 5 or 6 hours or overnight. Strain and chill until needed. Serve the tea with a simple syrup, lemon quarters, and lots of ice. To make a simple syrup, boil 2 parts of granulated sugar to 1 part of water for 5 minutes, stirring constantly.

ᐁ CHICKEN-LIVER PÂTÉ

The picnic that Sarah Bernhardt took aloft in her first ascension by balloon, unscheduled and unauthorized by her frantic manager below, is far better than any food I have ever had in the air; and such a picnic tastes equally well on the ground. Her basket was filled with pâté, French bread, champagne, and oranges.

1 lb. chicken livers
4 tablespoons softened unsalted butter
¼ cup sherry
¼ cup brandy
salt
1 fat clove garlic, minced
2 or more tablespoons butter
1 teaspoon Miss Leslie's kitchen pepper*
3 tablespoons shelled salted pistachios
or 2 tablespoons green peppercorns

Cut the chicken livers in half and sauté them in 2 tablespoons of the butter until they are brown on the outside and still pink within. Remove from the heat and put in the blender with the sherry and brandy. Add salt, garlic, softened butter, and Miss Leslie's pepper. Blend until smooth. Remove from blender and add pistachios or green peppercorns. Spoon the mixture into two crocks, each holding about a cup, and chill until firm. This is much better if made a day or two ahead of time. I suggest two crocks instead of one, for pure convenience.

Serve with hot toast or French bread and the rest of Sarah Bernhardt's menu if you like.

❧ PAN BAGNA

This is a wonderfully good sandwich that is all things to all people in the south of France, whether eaten by workmen or beautiful people on the beach.

French bread, about a foot for each person
2 large onions, peeled and sliced
2 green peppers, cut into strips
3 tablespoons olive oil
black olives
anchovies
more olive oil

Split the bread and fill it lavishly with the onions and peppers, drenched in olive oil, and the black olives and anchovies. Sprinkle with more olive oil. Eat it blissfully and messily in your hands, and accompany it with some good red wine.

Serve with watercress; green and purple grapes; cheese.

❧ SHISH KEBAB

I have been served shish kebab by a beautiful and brilliant Armenian woman in a well-equipped kitchen and by a gentle and charming Persian artist who cooked it skewer by skewer over a gas flame in a New York apartment. Each time it was a wondrously aromatic dish, but cooked outdoors over a charcoal grill on a terrace or at a picnic site, it tastes even better. This is Davoud Yonan's version with brandy in the marinade. Carry it to the picnic still in its marinade in a tightly covered bowl. Put the meat on skewers while the fire is getting to the right point. My skewers are the no-nonsense long sharp steel skewers with comfortable wooden handles that have traveled along with me for many years. They are still available at most stores carrying Near Eastern foods and cooking equipment. (Most of the skewers sold in the usual culinary equipment places are apt not to be as functionally designed.) When cooked at home, shish kebab can be served with Armenian pilaf*. At picnics, I omit the pilaf and serve with pideh*, the flat Near Eastern bread that sometimes I buy and sometimes I make.

> *2 lbs. young lamb, cut from the leg into 2-inch squares*
> *2 tablespoons lemon juice*
> *⅓ cup olive oil*
> *1 large onion, sliced thin*
> *1 tablespoon chopped fresh tarragon or 1 teaspoon dried*
> *1 teaspoon chopped fresh oregano or ½ teaspoon dried*
> *1 jigger brandy*
> *salt, pepper*
> *1 lb. fresh mushrooms, caps only*
> *1 lb. small fresh tomatoes, cut in quarters*

Put the pieces of lamb in a large bowl. Mix the lemon juice, olive oil, onion, tarragon, oregano, brandy, salt, and pepper and pour over the meat. Put in the refrigerator overnight. Turn the pieces of lamb from time to time and stir around so all the pieces become well marinated. Before cooking, remove the bowl from the refrigerator and let it come to room temperature. (This will take about 1 hour.) Put a piece of meat on each skewer followed by a piece of mushroom and a quarter of tomato, and repeat until all the skewers are loaded loosely. Broil over a charcoal grill, or one at a time over an open fire, indoors or out, or on top of the stove; they can also, of course, be cooked in a broiler. The mushrooms and the tomatoes should be browned and blistered, but still slightly raw. After broiling, push the meat and vegetables off the skewers onto a large, warm pottery platter. Serves 4.

Serve with pideh; a mixed green salad; orange-peel ice*; crisp chocolate cookies*.*

◄§ ROCK CORNISH HEN
WITH PARSLEY-AND-LEMON STUFFING

This is a fine dish for a picnic, where one can pick it up and eat it with one's fingers. There should be one bird for each person. I prefer them on picnics because they are neat, generous, and easier to eat than they are at the table.

6 Rock Cornish hens, about 1 lb. each
salt, pepper
1½ cups dried breadcrumbs
3 tablespoons lemon juice
1 teaspoon grated lemon rind
2 tablespoons finely chopped parsley
1 teaspoon dried marjoram
4 tablespoons melted butter
1 egg
more salt and freshly ground pepper

Wash and drain well the inside cavities of the hens and sprinkle with salt and pepper. Mix together the dried breadcrumbs, lemon juice, lemon rind, parsley, marjoram, and 3 tablespoons of the butter. Stir in the whole egg and mix well with your hands. Fill the cavities with the mixture but do not pack it in. Skewer close with pastry nails. Rub the outsides with the remaining butter and sprinkle with a bit of salt and pepper. Lay the birds on their sides and bake in a preheated 450° oven for 15 to 20 minutes until browned on top. Turn them to the other side and cook until done, another 20 minutes. When pricked with a fork in the thigh, the juice that runs out should be clear and yellow, not pink. Serves 6.

Serve with French bread; broccoli vinaigrette*; fresh ripe pears; Swiss Emmenthaler cheese.

✑ CHESAPEAKE PIE

In these days of sophisticated picnicking, this dish, served lukewarm and accompanied by a cold white wine such as a Muscadet or a Vouvray, is unusually satisfying. A deep-dish seafood pie, it is traditionally made with seasoned layers of crab meat and oysters, but it tastes equally good with any other combination of shellfish—shrimp and clams or mussels and crab meat. The baking dish must be at least 2 inches deep, so a 2-quart casserole or soufflé dish is better than a pie pan. The top crust is usually decorated with a ring of balls made of chopped oysters, breadcrumbs, and mashed hard-boiled egg yolk, seasoned with salt, pepper, mace, and nutmeg and fried in butter.

Pastry, enough for 3 9-inch crusts
1 lb. crab meat, picked over
¼ teaspoon red pepper
1 tablespoon grated lemon rind
3 hard-boiled egg yolks, mashed
¾ cup (1½ sticks) butter, softened
1 pint oysters, drained (reserve 1 cup of the liquor)
salt, pepper
1 pinch mace
1 pinch nutmeg
4 tablespoons flour
1 cup light cream or milk

Roll out two pastry circles, one slightly larger than the other. Line the casserole or soufflé dish with the larger pastry. Put half the crab meat in a layer on the bottom. Mix the red pepper, lemon rind, egg yolks, and 1 stick of butter together and dot half of the mixture on top of the crab meat. Next, make a layer of half the oysters. Cream together the remaining ½ stick of butter, salt, pepper, mace, nutmeg, and flour and crumble half of this mixture over the oysters. Make another layer of crab meat and its butter mixture; then add the rest of the oysters and their butter mixture. Mix the oyster liquor and the cream together and pour over the casserole. Cover with the top crust, prick it, and put in an oven preheated to 425°.   Bake for 25 minutes, until crust is well browned.   Serves 8.

Serve with cucumber and watercress salad with oil-and-lemon dressing; honeydew melon.

ᐸᔧ FISH MOUSSE

This meal for summer is a sensual and visual delight, for the mousse is both velvety in texture and subtle in flavoring.   The smooth, white mold is flecked with green, and the coral shrimp and the over-lapping circles of dark-rimmed pale green cucumbers make one feel cool, serene, and relaxed just to look at it.   It also tastes good if you can bear to break up the mold.

½ lb. cooked shrimp
½ cup olive oil
¼ cup lemon juice
salt, pepper
1 lb. cut-up fillet of halibut
2 cups white wine
½ lemon, sliced thin
1 small onion, sliced
2 envelopes unflavored gelatin
½ cup heavy cream, whipped
1 cup mayonnaise
½ cup finely chopped parsley
1 tablespoon salt
1 tablespoon dry mustard
1 tablespoon freshly grated horseradish
or 2 tablespoons of the prepared horseradish
1 long or 2 medium-sized cucumbers

Marinate the shrimp in the oil, lemon juice, salt, and pepper for 1 hour or more.   Poach the fish in 1 cup of the wine, 1 cup water, the lemon, and the onion, until the fish is opaque.   Let cool in the liquid.

Remove and discard the bones and skin. Put the fish in the blender, a little at a time, with the strained cooking liquid, and blend until it is smooth, or use a food mill. Soften the gelatin in the other cup of wine and heat it briefly until dissolved. Mix with the blended fish mixture and add the whipped cream, mayonnaise, parsley, and seasonings. When thoroughly mixed, turn into an oiled 1-quart ring mold. Chill until firm.

Unmold by dipping the mold briefly into hot water and running a knife around the edges to loosen them. Place the serving platter on top and invert it carefully. Fill the center with the marinated shrimp, drained. Run the tines of the fork down the sides of the unpeeled cucumber to make ridges. Slice the cucumbers very thin and arrange them in overlapping slices around the mold. This may be done several hours before serving and kept in the refrigerator. Serves 8.

Serve with hot mushroom broth; grapefruit Alaska*.

⋐§ PARSLEYED HAM

Aside from a beautiful whole baked ham, this Burgundian Easter dish (called jambon persillé by the French) is to my taste one of the most blissful ways of preparing and serving ham. The better the ham, the better the dish. It can be started with salted and cured fresh pork, cooked with pigs' feet and calves' feet (which produces a wonderfully flavored and delicate jelly). This modified version assumes that you have a *good* cooked ham or Canadian bacon in one piece and some good chicken or beef stock or broth.

2 envelopes unflavored gelatin
¼ cup bourbon or applejack (not obligatory)
3 cups homemade beef or chicken broth or stock
3 cups diced, cooked or canned ham
1 cup finely chopped fresh parsley
salt, pepper, if necessary (the ham and broth have some)

Soften the gelatin in the bourbon or applejack or equal amount of cold water. Pour into the broth and heat, stirring until completely dissolved. Remove from the heat and let it cool until it reaches the thickness of raw egg whites. Have ready a solid-colored bowl or deep platter, without any distracting designs. Put one layer of the ham in the bowl or platter. Add the parsley to the slightly thickened jelly. Pour a layer over the ham, add more ham, and so on until all the ingredients are used. The jelly should fill all the cracks and corners of the meat. It is preferable but not necessary to weight this dish with a heavy plate or heavy unopened can. This makes it easier to serve. Chill in the refrigerator until ready to serve. Cut in wedges and serve from the bowl. Serves 6 to 8.

Serve with spoon bread*; watercress and arugula salad with oil-and-vinegar dressing; glazed oranges*.

A Discrimination of Rice and Pasta

All around the world rice is eaten around the clock, by the rich and the poor, the young and the old, on feast days and on fast days. Variously cooked and seasoned, it is the basic food of more than half the earth's population.

Rice is all things to all meals—except, I insist stubbornly (despite some reputable opposition), for salads. What other food may be served at breakfast (in griddle cakes, muffins, breads); in soup; in appetizers and hors d'oeuvre; in light dishes such as eggs pilaf; in main meat dishes (Greek meat balls, jambalayas, and lots more); in curries, stuffings, and vegetable dishes; and in interesting and ambrosial desserts. Rice can also be served in the form of wine—as in Japanese sake—and at weddings in many countries it is thrown at the bride and groom to ensure them fertility.

Rice is inexpensive, easy to store, and needs no fussy or tedious preparations. Some of the simplest ways of cooking rice are the best of all. For example, put 1 cup of raw unwashed rice into a pot with 2 cups of beef or chicken stock, ½ teaspoon salt (most stock is salty, so don't overdo it), and 1 small onion, finely chopped. Bring to a boil, cover, lower heat, and cook for 20 minutes until the stock is absorbed. Fluff with a fork and serve with a lump of butter on top. The rice will have a subtle flavor of stock, and the bits of onion will give a nice textural contrast to the rice.

Pasta, often used as a alternate to rice, is not as universal a food but is infinitely more varied—at least in shape. The ingredients are usually the same—flour, water, salt, and sometimes eggs—but it is made in thick and thin strips, bows, shells, tubes, plain or grooved, and more. Molded, dried in strings, and then cooked in lots of boiling water, pasta is most common in Italy, but can be found in the

151

native cuisines of France, Austria, Hungary, China, and elsewhere. Pasta can be dressed simply and perfectly with butter and freshly grated cheese, with red or white clam sauce, with a combination of oil, garlic, and walnuts. It can also be baked with spinach and one of several different sauces for a fine and simple light supper or as an accompaniment to an important meat dish. Greeks take a macaroni pie called pastichio along with them on picnics to eat at air temperature.

Most of the sauces that Italians eat with pasta are equally good with polenta, a cornmeal dish that our Southerners call mush and Rumanians call mamaliga.

Those who love dumplings in stews are a devoted lot, but such high-bulk foods tend to make me feel overstuffed even before I start to eat them. I much prefer a light dumpling such as spaetzle, which is closer to pasta than the biscuit dumplings served in this country.

⋙ CHILI WITH RED BEANS AND RICE

When I was young and wrote my first cookbook, I had never known a Texan, and I worked out a recipe for chili that used cubed beef rather than ground. I still prefer it that way. Since then many Texans have given me recipes for "absolutely authentic" chili, using ground beef. The red beans, traditionally served on the side, not in the chili, are often cooked with rice. This decorative version involving a rice ring with chili beans in the center is derived from a recipe in Thomas Jefferson's cookbook and is not Texan at all.

2½ lbs. round steak or chuck, cut in 1½-inch cubes
¼ cup fat from steak, chopped
2 tablespoons olive oil
3 scallions, tops and bottoms, chopped
2 cloves garlic, chopped
¼ cup, more or less, good chili powder
1 teaspoon powdered cumin
salt, freshly ground pepper
2 cups or more beef stock

In a large skillet brown the meat and fat from the steak in the olive oil. Add the scallions and garlic, sprinkle with seasonings, and add the beef stock. Bring the mixture to a boil, cover, turn the heat down low and simmer for several hours. The exact amount of time doesn't matter. It may be done the day before and allowed to "ripen" in the refrigerator; it may also be frozen. If frozen, the seasonings must be checked and some fresh chili powder and freshly chopped scallions added before reheating. Serves 8.

Serve with a ring mold of rice cooked in chicken broth, its center filled with canned kidney beans heated with ¼ lb. diced scalded salt pork, pepper, and 1 teaspoon oregano (drain before adding to the ring mold of rice); sliced avocado and grapefruit salad; French bread.

⊷§ PICADILLO WITH RICE AND BEANS

A fine Spanish mishmash of meat and raisins, and sometimes olives and nuts, usually served with rice and beans. The beans can be garbanzos, or chickpeas, pink Mexican beans, red kidney beans, or, handsomest of all, black beans. Usually the black beans must be bought dried and soaked and simmered with a ham hock until tender, but increasingly they can be found canned in sections of the country where Hispanic people live.

1 medium onion, minced
1 clove garlic, minced
4 tablespoons olive oil
1½ lbs. chopped beef
2 cups canned tomatoes
2 tablespoons raisins
1 teaspoon dry hot chili pepper
1 teaspoon vinegar
salt, pepper
4 cups cooked rice
3 cups cooked black or other beans
1 hard-cooked egg white, chopped
½ cup slivered almonds

Sauté the onion and garlic in the olive oil in a large skillet. Add the beef, tomatoes, raisins, chili pepper, vinegar, salt, and pepper. Simmer over a low heat for about 30 minutes. Although this is called a stew, it is served rather dry over fluffy white rice, with black beans or other beans on the side. Sprinkle the top of the stew with chopped hard-cooked egg white and almonds. Serves 4 to 6.

Serve with watercress and grapefruit salad with French dressing; hot rolls; flan.

✒ ARMENIAN PILAF

This pilaf, prepared with care and pride, involves a somewhat different technique than that of an Italian risotto but gives equally happy results. This may be prepared several hours ahead of time and kept warm.

¼ lb. butter
1 cup uncooked rice
1 large onion, chopped (often omitted)
2 cups chicken broth
salt and pepper, if necessary

Melt the butter in a heavy saucepan and add the uncooked rice and onion, if used. Stir around until the rice is coated and pale yellow. Add the chicken broth and additional seasoning if necessary. Cover and cook over a very low heat 20 to 25 minutes, or until the rice is tender. The Armenians and Turks then remove the cover and put a clean napkin over the top of the pot to absorb any moisture, then cover again. To reheat, stir a bit over a low fire. It seldom needs any more liquid because this amount of butter keeps it moist. Serves 4.

Serve with parsleyed chicken*; Persian mäst*; grapefruit Alaska*.

◦§ TURKISH PILAF

A light, savory one-dish meal. Try to find the imported tomato paste that comes in a tube, which is convenient for dishes that use just a tablespoon or more. It is not widely distributed but worth the effort.

1 cup raw long-grain rice
¼ cup butter, plus 2 tablespoons
1 tablespoon pine nuts or pignolias
½ cup chopped onions
3 tablespoons chopped sweet pepper, preferably red
2 cups chicken broth
salt, pepper
1 teaspoon ground allspice
1 teaspoon grated lemon rind
1 tablespoon tomato paste
3 tablespoons golden seedless raisins
½ lb. chicken livers, quartered

In a deep heavy saucepan cook the rice in ¼ cup of the butter until translucent. Add the pine nuts, chopped onions, and pepper and cook for a few minutes before adding chicken broth, salt, pepper, allspice, lemon rind, tomato paste, and raisins. Bring to a boil, cover, and cook over a low heat for 20 to 25 minutes. In the meantime sauté the chicken livers in the remaining 2 tablespoons of butter. Stir these into the pilaf and transfer to a serving dish. Serves 4.

Serve with Persian mast*; orange-peel ice*; crisp chocolate cookies*.

◦§ CHICKEN LIVERS IN WHITE-WINE SAUCE WITH WILD RICE

Wild rice is, to me, still a richly satisfying grain, and richly is the operative word. It is expensive and lends panache to an otherwise simple dish. There is a good commercial and considerably less expensive blend of wild rice and brown rice.

1 cup wild rice, well-washed
3 cups chicken broth, or more
1 lb. chicken livers, each cut in 3 or 4 pieces
2 tablespoons bacon fat
2 tablespoons flour
salt, pepper
½ cup red or white wine

Cook the rice in 2 cups of the chicken broth. (There should be enough broth to cover the rice; add more if rice starts to dry out.) Bring to a boil, cover, and simmer over low heat for 50 to 60 minutes, or until the rice is tender and the liquid absorbed. Fluff with a fork. For the sauce, sauté the chicken livers in the fat until brown. Remove the livers from the pan; blend the flour and seasonings into the fat and slowly add the wine and the remaining broth. When the sauce is smooth, return the chicken livers to the pan. Put the rice on the bottom of a medium-sized shallow casserole and pour the chicken livers and sauce over the top. Bake in a 350° oven for 20 minutes. Serves 4.

Serve with Belgian endive salad with oil-and-vinegar dressing; French bread cut in chunks, with sweet butter; lemon soufflé*.

❧ SHRIMP AND WILD-RICE SALAD

Fundamentally, I am against rice salad as I am against macaroni salad. Nonetheless, this combination of shrimp and wild rice—or a wild-rice blend if you are feeling frugal—is a different thing entirely.

1 cup wild rice or 1 cup white and wild rice mixed
1 cup sliced raw mushrooms
2 tablespoons vegetable or olive oil
2 tablespoons lemon juice
1 lb. peeled, deveined, and cooked shrimp
1 green pepper, seeded and chopped
1 cup aioli*

2 *hard-cooked eggs*
watercress

Cook the wild rice or wild-rice mixture in 2 cups of salted water until tender, about 30 minutes. Drain and chill. Dress the rice and the mushrooms with the oil and lemon juice. Add the shrimp, green pepper, and aioli and mix loosely. Coarsely chop the egg whites and sieve the yolks. Garnish the salad with the eggs and watercress. Serves 4.

Serve with crusty French bread; grapefruit Alaska*.

⊰ PORK CHOPS WITH SOUR CHERRIES

A surprisingly simple, unexpected combination that appeals to many, *even* the unadventurous.

4 *thick loin pork chops*
1 *cup uncooked rice*
2 *cups canned sour cherries*
1 *tablespoon sugar*
grated rind of ½ lemon
1 *teaspoon cinnamon*
salt, pepper

Brown the pork chops on both sides in their own fat. Place the rice in the bottom of a deep casserole or Dutch oven; pour the cherries and their juice over it, plus ⅔ cup water. Sprinkle the sugar, lemon rind, and cinnamon over this and arrange the pork chops on top. Salt and pepper to taste and cover. Bake in a 350° oven for 1 hour or until liquid is absorbed. Lift the chops and fluff the rice with a fork. Replace and serve. Serves 4.

Serve with salad of thin slices of sweet Bermuda onion pulled into rings, lettuce, and oil-and-lemon dressing; round Italian bread; lemon granita*.

✒ PARCHED RICE WITH DRIED CHERRIES

This rice dish comes from a Chinese man who cooked for my husband's family on the island of Kauai, in Hawaii, long ago. The parching or toasting may be done ahead of time and gives a nutty, different taste and appearance to ordinary long-grain rice. Dried cherries, which are usually found in Near Eastern food stores, have pits but a flavor well worth the bother of eating them. When dried cherries are not available, use either canned pitted black Bing cherries or sour red cherries drained.

1½ cups Carolina long-grain rice
½ cup dried cherries, soaked and drained
3 cups chicken broth, or less
½ cup chopped scallions
½ cup slivered almonds
¼ cup melted butter
salt, freshly ground pepper

Toast the rice by shaking or stirring in a dry skillet over a low heat until it turns a nice light toast color. Add the cherries, using their soaking or canned liquid and enough chicken broth to make up 3 cups. Add the scallions and almonds and bring to a boil. Cover, turn the heat down, and simmer for 30 or more minutes. This dish requires slightly longer cooking than plain rice, but not much. Remove from the heat and fluff with a fork. Add the melted butter, salt and pepper. Serves 4 to 6.

Serve with parsleyed chicken*; sliced cucumbers with vinaigrette dressing; chocolate mousse*.

✒ RASPBERRY RICE

A fortuitous and happy assemblage apparently invented in Central Europe. It is really a lighter and simpler variation of the English trifle.

> 1 cup cold boiled rice
> ⅓ cup sugar
> 1 cup fresh or frozen raspberries
> 1 jigger Cointreau
> ½ cup heavy cream, whipped

Mix or toss lightly all the ingredients together just before serving. Serves 4.

Serve after carbonnade*; spaetzle*; raw mushroom salad* with water-cress.

✌ᢥ SPAETZLE

The simplest of all pastas to make and cook at home, spaetzle are tiny dumplings often served in Austria, Hungary, and other Central European countries. It is not the traditional pasta to serve with pesto*, but they go well together. Spaetzle is also good served with just butter and breadcrumbs, or with sour cream and butter, and it makes an excellent addition to homemade soup.

> 1½ cups all-purpose flour
> ¼ teaspoon salt
> 2 eggs
> ½ cup milk
> ½ cup water
> ¼ lb. butter
> breadcrumbs (optional)

Put the flour, salt, eggs, milk, and water in the blender and blend briefly. The batter should be smooth and soft but not stiff. Turn it out onto a chopping board. Cut the mixture into small pieces about the size of shelled almonds. Put them directly into boiling salted water and boil for a few minutes. Drain them in a colander, pour cold water over them, and drain again. Brown the spaetzle in a hot skillet with the butter, adding brown buttered crumbs if desired. If being served with pesto*, omit the browning and the buttered crumbs but keep the spaetzle warm after draining. Add the pesto at room temperature.

Serve with broiled chicken halves; cold broccoli vinaigrette*; raspberry rice*.

~ SCHNITZ UND KNEPP
(DRIED APPLES AND DUMPLINGS)

Although I grew up with a cook from Lancaster, Pennsylvania, I never had this dish until years later when I was doing a story on Pennsylvania Dutch cooking. I was especially taken with the quartered dried apples, which I like better than thin, less juicy circles of dried apples. The recipe for the dumplings, or knepp, is given here as they cook it. I also prefer the less doughy spaetzle* with this dish, but those with lustier appetites will like the knepp.

2 cups dried apples
2 lbs. smoked ham cut in chunks or 2 or 3 ham hocks
2 tablespoons brown sugar
3 or more cups water or, preferably, cider
2 cups flour
2 teaspoons baking powder
½ teaspoon salt
1 egg, beaten
2 tablespoons of melted butter
⅔ cup milk

Put the dried apples, smoked ham or ham hocks, and sugar together in a Dutch oven or a heavy pot with a tight-fitting cover. Cover with water or cider depending upon how lavish you feel. Bring to a boil, cover tightly, and turn heat down. Simmer until the ham is tender, about 1½ to 2 hours. Mix the flour, baking powder, salt, egg, butter, and milk together for the dumplings.

If you are using ham hocks, remove them when tender. Skin them and cut the meat from the bones, cut it into chunks, and return to the liquid. Bring the liquid to a boil and drop teaspoonfuls of the dumpling mixture into the liquid. Cover tightly and cook for 20 minutes without looking. If you are using spaetzle*, cook according to directions given under that recipe. Serves 4 to 6 generously.

Serve with red cole slaw with Roquefort dressing and, traditionally, lemon meringue pie.*

⊷§ KASHA

Kasha, or buckwheat groats, is one of the blessings of Russian and Polish cuisine. It is a nutritious addition to our cuisine and is now increasingly available in American food stores. Be sure to get whole-grain kasha because the ground versions are apt to be a bit mushy. The following is the classic way of cooking kasha, although it may of course be adapted to other techniques.

1 large egg
1 cup kasha or whole-grain brown buckwheat groats
1 teaspoon salt
2 cups chicken broth
2 tablespoons butter or rendered chicken fat

Beat the egg lightly with a fork just long enough for the yolk and white to blend. Put the kasha in a small heavy skillet. Add the egg and stir until the kasha is coated and the egg is no longer visible. Toast over moderate heat until the grains begin to separate and give off a pleasant odor. When the skillet is hot, add the salt and the broth and stir in the butter or fat. Cover and reduce heat (or bake, covered, in a 350° oven). Steam for 30 to 45 minutes, checking now and then, and adding more broth if the kasha becomes too dry. Fluff with a fork. Serves 4.

Serve with lamb chops; Italian green bean salad; orange-peel ice*.*

·§ SPAGHETTI ALLA CARBONARA

Much as I enjoy some of the good, long-cooking Italian sauces for pasta, I have a marked preference for the lighter sauces that are cooked relatively briefly.

4 tablespoons salt
4 thick slices lean salt pork, cut in fine dice
4 tablespoons olive oil
3 eggs, slightly beaten
¼ cup dry white wine
½ cup mixed freshly grated Parmesan and Romano cheese
1 lb. spaghetti (Italian imported, if possible)
freshly ground black pepper
2 tablespoons finely chopped parsley

Heat 4 quarts of water with the 4 tablespoons of salt until boiling. Meanwhile, sauté the lean salt pork in the olive oil. Mix the eggs, white wine, and cheese together and add the diced pork with some of the fat. Cook the spaghetti in the boiling water until soft but not mushy. Remove and drain. Transfer to a heated platter and pour the pork and egg mixture onto the spaghetti. Toss rapidly and thoroughly until the pasta is thoroughly coated with the mixture. The heat of the pasta and platter should be hot enough to half cook the eggs. Sprinkle with the freshly ground black pepper and parsley. Serve at once. Serves 4.

Serve with mixed green salad; orange-peel ice*.

⊷§ LASAGNE WITH SPINACH

The first book I bought in Paris long ago was Ali Bab's *Gastronomie Pratique*. It is a fascinating and huge book with imaginative and sometimes inspired variations on classic combinations. This is freely adapted from his recipe. As he says, it lacks banality.

½ lb. lasagne, homemade or bought
2 lbs. fresh spinach or 2 10-oz. packages frozen spinach
⅓ cup butter
1½ cups good meat stock or consommé
1¼ cups freshly grated Parmesan cheese
salt, if necessary
freshly ground black pepper

Cook the lasagne in a 4-quart pot of boiling salted water 5 to 8 minutes for homemade, 10 to 12 for bought, or until tender but not mushy. Drain well. Meanwhile cook the fresh spinach for 5 to 10 minutes in salted water (less for frozen). Drain well, chop, and mix with the butter, meat stock, and 1 cup of the grated cheese, salt, and pepper. Arrange a layer of half the lasagne in a shallow baking dish. Spread half the spinach mixture over the top and layer with the rest of the lasagne. Top with the remaining spinach. Sprinkle evenly with the remaining ¼ cup of the cheese. Bake in a preheated 350° oven for 30 to 45 minutes or until hot, bubbling, and lightly browned. Serves 4 to 6.

Serve with Black Forest ham or another good-flavored variety; cherry tomatoes; lemon granita*.

A Succulence of Salads

One of the loveliest of all dishes is a fresh green salad glistening with oil and vinegar or lemon, what the French call salade verte or salade de saison. Such a dish should not be difficult to make, yet few people I know do manage to come up with distinguished salads, even those who are skilled in the kitchen.

Given good ingredients, the element that seems to make the difference between mediocrity and excellence is getting the fresh, crisp greens properly dry. It is not easy to remove all the moisture, but if it is not removed, the dressing will be diluted and the greens will be limp. It doesn't matter how the drying is accomplished. One method preferred by a superb cook who was an aunt of my husband's is to put the greens in a dish towel and whirl it around one's head (out of doors, of course), or you can whirl the greens—over a deep sink—in a French wire salad basket. One can blot the greens carefully with paper towels before chilling them in a plastic bag, but most people are not patient enough to get *all* the moisture out.

Although I dislike overmechanized kitchens, I make an exception in the case of a gadget called a salad drier or spin drier. Made of plastic with nothing to get out of order, this truly works miracles, even getting a half cup or more of water from greens you thought were well drained. If the washing and drying are done as soon as you bring the greens home, and they are stored in a plastic bag in the refrigerator, they will be handy for last-minute use, and will keep longer than greens washed in the old-fashioned way.

These days there is a wide and happy selection of greens available in most markets. How well I remember the bad old days when nothing but iceberg lettuce could be found except in very large cities. Although it stores well, iceberg lettuce is as flavorless to me as cottony

164

supermarket bread. I usually prefer to use two or three different greens at a time, although a good crisp watercress is sufficient by itself. Margaret Bourke-White, in her autobiography, recalls that there was great competition among her photographer friends to see who could find the largest variety of greens. She was delighted at one point when she was able to find and use nineteen in one salad!

There are many enticing greens to be found or grown—the pretty red oak-leaf lettuce, the delicate pale leaf lettuce, spicy watercress, the slender yellowish white heads of what we call Belgian endive, but what is known in that country and in England as chicory. What we call chicory, they call endive. I also like small, buttery heads of Bibb lettuce, and salads made of arugula (called raquette by the French) with its haunting musty flavor.

Any good, fresh (meaning not rancid) oil may be used. I use a good brand of olive oil, sometimes French, sometimes Italian, and more recently, Spanish. If I am expecting a guest who is on a very strict low-cholesterol diet, I use an unsaturated fat with just a table-spoon of olive oil to flavor it. From time to time I also use a sesame-seed oil; the Middle Eastern variety has a delicate flavor, the Oriental a more gutsy taste. I buy these in small amounts and store them in the refrigerator, letting them come to room temperature before using.

I am apt to have several different types of vinegars on hand at any given time. Tarragon white vinegar, red wine vinegar, and cider vinegar are standard, but occasionally I use a slightly sweet rice vinegar. What I prefer most in a dressing, however, and what delights my guests the most, is fresh lemon juice instead of the vinegar. The proportions I like are four parts of oil to one part of lemon juice (or vinegar) with a pinch of sea salt used cautiously, since it is more emphatic than kitchen salt, and freshly ground pepper. What is added from then on depends on my mood and my supplies—a few fresh herbs, fresh sliced mushrooms, garlic, mustard, bits of cooked bacon or anchovy, or whatever seasoning seems to complement the rest of the meal. I use only one or two of these at a time, or none at all. The best salad maker I have known measured her oil in a bowl about a half an hour before using and put a salted garlic clove in it. After making her dressing, she fished out the garlic clove and discarded it. This method works better than simply rubbing a salad bowl with a clove of garlic, which does nothing at all to season the salad. Then the dried, chilled, and torn salad greens were delicately tossed in the oil until each leaf glistened. At the last minute she sprinkled the salad with vinegar or lemon juice, salt, and other seasonings, and it was always superb.

I usually measure, mix, and season my dressing ahead of time while the greens chill separately. Just before serving I put the greens into the salad bowl, give the dressing another stir, and sprinkle it over the greens, lifting and stirring so that they and the dressing get well mingled. When you are serving one of the many composed salads that appear throughout this book, I suggest that you make the dressing in this way, but sprinkle it on the arranged salad without tossing.

Another dressing that I use frequently with light greens such as Bibb or leaf lettuce I learned from a Danish friend (and a similar version from someone of Pennsylvania Dutch extraction). Simply mix ½ cup of heavy cream with 1 teaspoon lemon juice, a pinch of sea salt, and some freshly ground black pepper. It also makes a very good slaw, when you substitute shredded cabbage for lettuce.

～§ ITALIAN GREEN BEAN SALAD

This is one of my favorite vegetable salads and can be made from foods easily kept on hand. It is a good salad to have when fresh greens are not around or are deplorably unfresh. It is also a good salad for a solitary meal.

1 package frozen Italian green beans
½ cup canned, drained mandarin oranges
1 whole canned pimiento, cut in large pieces about 1-inch square
2 scallions, trimmed and chopped
½ teaspoon dried oregano
3 tablespoons olive oil
2 teaspoons lemon juice
salt, freshly ground black pepper

Cook the Italian green beans according to directions until they are barely tender and still crisp. Drain and arrange on a small plain-colored pottery platter. Strew the oranges, pimiento, and scallions over the beans. Mix the oregano, olive oil, lemon juice, salt and pepper together with a fork and pour it over the beans and oranges. This is best served at room temperature, but it may be made ahead of time and chilled if wished. Serves 4 with the main dish. To serve as a luncheon dish, double the recipe for 4.

Serve with cheese and smoked-oyster soufflé*; glazed oranges*.

BROCCOLI VINAIGRETTE

This is equally good served hot or cold.

> *1 bunch fresh broccoli*
> *1 small clove garlic*
> *½ teaspoon Dijon mustard*
> *2 tablespoons wine vinegar*
> *1 pinch salt*
> *1 pinch freshly ground black pepper*
> *½ cup salad oil*

Cook the broccoli in boiling salted water until tender. Remove, drain, and break into flowerets. Chill, or keep warm, as desired. Put the garlic clove, mustard, vinegar, salt, pepper, and oil in the container of the blender. Blend briefly until well mixed. Pour over the broccoli. Serves 4.

Serve with Persian red beans*; lemon granita*.

✥ RED COLE SLAW
WITH ROQUEFORT DRESSING

This robust salad is best served with a sturdy main dish such as
one of the bean casseroles.

3 cups coarsely chopped red cabbage
1 cup sour cream
2 tablespoons white wine vinegar or lemon juice
¼ cup orange juice
¼ cup crumbled Roquefort or other blue cheese
no salt, no pepper

Put the chopped cabbage in a rough natural-colored pottery or
glass bowl. Mix the sour cream, vinegar, and orange juice with a
wire whisk or fork. Stir in the crumbled Roquefort and pour over
the cabbage. Serves 4 to 6.

Serve with chile con carne*; coffee granita*.

✥ FRESH SPINACH WITH SESAME PASTE

This could be served either as an appetizer or as a salad.

1 lb. fresh spinach, washed and picked over
2 tablespoons soy sauce
1 tablespoon sesame paste

Take a bunch of the spinach and dip it into boiling water until
it becomes limp. Repeat the procedure with another bunch until
all the spinach has been used. Lay the bunches together and
squeeze, draining off all the excess water. Cut the spinach into
2-inch lengths. Dribble a little soy sauce over the spinach and put
a dollop of sesame paste on top. If you can't find sesame paste in
your local market, make some by toasting sesame seeds in a medium

hot skillet until they jump. Mash them to a paste with a sprinkle of sugar and a bit of soy sauce.

ᴥᔡ CAESAR SALAD

This is a pleasing version of a classic dish.

romaine or escarole
½ cup crumbled Roquefort cheese
½ cup freshly grated Parmesan cheese
croutons
¼ cup olive oil
1 clove garlic, peeled and left whole
1 egg (optional though usual)
olive oil for dressing
lemon juice
Worcestershire sauce
salt, freshly ground black pepper

Wash and dry the greens and tear them into pieces into a salad bowl. Crumble the Roquefort and sprinkle the Parmesan cheese over the greens. In a separate bowl toss the croutons in ¼ cup olive oil and the garlic and add them to the salad. Cook the egg for a minute if you wish, or leave it raw, and break over the salad. Make the dressing by mixing 2 parts olive oil and 1 part lemon juice, the amount depending on the size of the salad, adding a dash or more of Worcestershire sauce, salt, and pepper. Pour over all, toss, and serve.

ᴥᔡ PERSIAN MÄST

Cucumbers, mint, and yogurt make a sublime combination for a salad, an accompaniment to curry, or a light dish for "private stomaching," a wonderful phrase from Shakespeare's *Antony and Cleopatra*.

1 cup plain yogurt
3 sprigs of fresh mint, chopped,
or ½ teaspoon of dried mint leaves
1 cucumber, peeled and chopped fine
1 scallion, trimmed and chopped
1 tablespoon golden seedless raisins
salt, freshly ground black pepper

Mix the ingredients together and chill for at least two hours before serving. Makes 2 cups.

Serve with parsleyed ham*; capellini*; frozen preserved ginger in whipped cream*.

ORANGE AND BLACK-OLIVE SALAD

Moroccan salads can be quite unlike our traditional salad fare. Some have no greens, others no oil and still others neither lemon juice nor vinegar, but all are agreeable and refreshing accompaniments to a meal.

3 navel or temple oranges
½ cup wrinkled, oil-cured black olives, pitted
2 tablespoons olive oil
pinch of cumin
pinch of cayenne
pinch of sugar
salt
2 tablespoons chopped fresh parsley

Peel the oranges, being certain to remove all bits of white. Over a serving bowl, cut into sections, collecting the juice with the sections. Add the black olives. Separately, mix a dressing of the olive oil and all the seasonings except the fresh parsley. Toss the dressing with the salad and sprinkle parsley over all. This dish is best when it is prepared ahead of time and allowed to marinate. Serve chilled or at room temperature. Serves 4.

Serve with meat loaf baked in a crust*; flageolets à la crème*; crème brûlée*.

ᴇᏡ TURKEY AND PINEAPPLE SALAD

An elegant way to present cooked turkey on a sunny spring day or even the day after Thanksgiving. Serve in clear glass bowls or plates and use pastel dining mats and napkins for some attractive contrasts.

2 cups cooked turkey breast, cut in julienne strips
1 cup fresh pineapple, cut in julienne strips
1 cup blueberries or sliced strawberries
1 cup mayonnaise
2 tablespoons fresh lemon juice
½ teaspoon honey

Mix the turkey, pineapple, and berries. Stir the mayonnaise, lemon juice, and honey together and pour onto the turkey and fruits. Divide and place on serving dishes. Serves 4.

Serve with sopaipillas*; Key lime pie*.

◄§ CURRIED CHICKEN SALAD
WITH CHERRIES AND BRAZIL NUTS

A long-time favorite of mine for a special luncheon on a hot day or for a Sunday-night supper.

3 cups diced cooked chicken (see recipe for poached chicken*)
¼ cup diced scallions
1 cup fresh or canned pitted black Bing cherries, drained
1 cup homemade or good commercial mayonnaise (not salad dressing)
1 teaspoon to 1 tablespoon curry powder to taste
watercress
½ cup Brazil-nut chips*

Mix the diced chicken, scallions, and Bing cherries together gently in a bowl. Season the mayonnaise with the curry powder to your taste and mix gently with the chicken and cherry mixture. Wash the watercress, dry it gently, and break off the stems. Strew the leaves in a plain glass or pottery bowl and heap the salad on top. Sprinkle with the Brazil-nut chips. Serves 4.

Serve with French bread; chocolate mousse*.

◄§ SALADE NIÇOISE

There is no special reason for still another recipe for this salad except that it is one of the best of all main-dish salads, easily assembled, and very popular. The only essential, traditional ingredients are tomatoes, beans, black olives, tuna or anchovies; potatoes, hard-cooked eggs, and capers are added or omitted according to personal whim.

3 good tomatoes, peeled, seeded, and quartered
½ cup cooked green string beans
½ cup wrinkled, oil-cured black olives (now available in cans)
1 6½- or 7-oz. can tuna fish

3 hard-cooked eggs, quartered
1 2-oz. can anchovies, cut in pieces
1 tablespoon capers
dressing (4 parts olive oil, 1 part vinegar,
salt, pepper, and ½ teaspoon Dijon mustard)

Toss or—somewhat untraditionally—arrange the ingredients in attractive concentric circles, and top with the dressing. Toss before serving or let your guests do so. In France this is served as an hors d'oeuvre, but at my place it is a main dish. Serves 4.

Serve with pideh*; glazed oranges*.

An Enhancement of Seasonings

I have read a good deal about the long and dangerous voyages to bring back spices from the Far East. These spices made fortunes for those who survived the voyages, because, at least for kings, queens, and those who could afford them, they made meat that had been butchered in the fall palatable all winter long. The most important of all the spices in those days was pepper, and this is still true, although pepper is no longer used for barter and to pay debts. As each new exotic spice was discovered and brought back, it became a highly desirable and costly luxury. Home-grown herbs, on the other hand, were for the peasants. One can only wonder why spices and herbs, once so essential to cooking, went so totally out of fashion in the nineteenth century. Was it the genteelism of the English and American Victorians, who believed that exciting and highly seasoned food was foreign and immoral, that any riot of any of the senses should be subdued and ignored? For many years most dishes (except desserts) were seasoned sedately with only salt and a tiny bit of pepper. There was a plethora of cream soups, creamed chicken, creamed lobster, creamed asparagus, creamed peas, creamed potatoes, and all manner of gelatin "salads." Oh, there were a few wayward exceptions, as always. Once in a while a clove of garlic might be daringly slipped into a dish, though it was usually frowned upon by "nice" people. And in desserts, cinnamon and clove might be used to spark up sugared fruit flavors.

The wonderfully tasty and textured dishes of our richly varied ethnic populations did not emerge visibly until well into the twentieth century, when it became fashionable to eat Italian food with drinks in speakeasies and delicatessen food in the theater district.

Little by little during the thirties, seasonings began to sneak into

174

printed recipes and trickle into conservative quality food stores, although they had always been available in the ethnic quarters of large cities. A few books on herbs were published, but the landmark publication of Irma Rombauer's aptly named *Joy of Cooking* in the mid-thirties impressed many generations of cooks with its excitingly seasoned dishes. It triggered the publication of many good specialty cookbooks over the next few years, and since then a torrent of books, articles, and columns on food has been flowing from the presses, some of which are distinguished in their research and writing, some mediocre and dull, others bad and silly.

Concurrently, the interest in all kinds of seasonings increased to an enormous extent, so that spices and herbs considered exotic thirty or so years ago can now be found in supermarkets throughout the land, even in remote areas.

A seasoning in my view is anything that adds flavor to food—not just the berries, roots, buds, flowers, pods, seeds, barks, and essences that we call spices, and the soft-stemmed green herbs, but also the juice and peel of oranges and lemons and other fruits, soy sauce and Chinese oyster sauce, vinegars, and the many different forms of sugars, salts, and peppers.

In spite of my enthusiasm for these varieties of seasonings, I do make some cautionary notes for those who wish to experiment. *Use them with restraint.* When you are following a recipe that calls for herbs or spices, taste before you serve. If you are adding herbs to a dish, use very little at first and gradually increase the quantity to your own taste. Some combinations can have surprising medicinal side effects. When we were very young, my husband and I concocted a fragrant and delicious rolled veal roast, generously sprinkled with a mixture of minced fresh herbs before we rolled it. Each slice looked very elegant with its green spiral of seasonings, but to our surprise it also acted as a strong cathartic that neither of us anticipated or needed.

Be sure to check the spices and herbs on your shelf every so often to make sure that they are still fresh. Because dried herbs can become stale, it is always better to buy small amounts. Some have a longer shelf age than others, but generally speaking, spices should be replaced at least once a year if not more often. Even when older, Jamaica ginger packaged in England is stronger than some current

American brands. Tellicherry peppercorns from the White Flower Farm in Litchfield, Connecticut, may keep fresh almost forever. Ground spices invariably keep less well than whole ones. Herbs vary more than spices do, even when they come from a good grower or packager. The process of drying often makes an herb stronger and more concentrated than its fresh counterpart, so keep this in mind when you make substitutions and adjust the quantity accordingly.

Proper curry is blended from many spices each time it is used, the proportions, quantities, and types of spices specially selected according to the food to be seasoned. Prepared curry powders are never entirely successful, although I do recall that some years ago, when I was living in Washington, I often saw Indian women in beautiful saris buying good Madras curry powder, although the separate spices were available. Try experimenting with different brands until you find one blend that you like, if you don't care to blend your own.

❧ MISS LESLIE'S KITCHEN PEPPER

Miss Leslie was one of the early Americans who cared about helping people to cook well and interestingly with the ingredients available to them. One of her inventions was this mixed seasoning that she called kitchen pepper. It adds zest to a stew, a soup, a pâté, or an oil-and-vinegar dressing when half a teaspoon is added to the dish.

2 tablespoons white powdered ginger
2 teaspoons black pepper
1 tablespoon ground cinnamon
1 tablespoon ground nutmeg
1 teaspoon ground cloves

Mix well. Keep in a tightly covered spice jar with the rest of your seasonings. Makes about ½ cup.

⋲§ PESTO GENOVESE

Pesto might well be the unanimous choice of pasta-loving food writers. It *must* be made with fresh basil, which some stores carry in season. Even if you live in the city, it is worth growing basil in window boxes or on the terrace. It is easy to grow, and the sauce freezes well if you freeze just the leaves and olive oil and add the other ingredients when ready to use. It can be made in the blender. It is traditionally added to minestrone, is perfect with pasta, is good on polenta and in a risotto.

> *2 cloves garlic*
> *1 cup crushed basil leaves*
> *½ cup freshly grated Parmesan or Pecorino or Sardo cheese*
> *½ cup olive oil*
> *⅓ cup pine nuts or pignolias or walnuts*

Put the garlic, basil, cheese, olive oil, and pine nuts in the blender. Blend until smooth. This may be kept in the refrigerator or in the freezer. For freezing, see note above. Makes 1 cup or slightly more.

Serve with hamburgers with lemon-and-egg sauce; pasta; bowl of cherry tomatoes; Key lime pie*.

⋲§ AIOLI GARNI

This dish is a fine debauch for those who enjoy the glorious reek of garlic, and guests invited for this meal must be as carefully selected as the garlic itself. Avoid that dreary, desiccated package stuff sold in supermarkets and look for heads of garlic with plump cloves and a slight tinge of pinkish lavender. (These are usually best in Italian stores offering good fresh produce.)

Make the aioli first before assembling your garni. It can be made in a blender, but this is frowned upon, although I do so when pressed for time. Serve the aioli in a bowl at room temperature to be spooned over the foods decoratively arranged on a platter. It can be a simple assortment for a few people or a grand production like that which the French serve on Christmas Eve.

8 cloves garlic
4 egg yolks
1 tablespoon or more fresh lemon juice
½ teaspoon salt
pinch of cayenne
1½ cups olive oil

Mash the peeled garlic in a large mortar with a pestle or mince it with a sharp knife. Stir in the egg yolks and beat with a wire whisk or a rotary beater. Add a tablespoon of boiling water, lemon juice, salt, and cayenne and beat well before adding the olive oil in small amounts. Add a teaspoon of oil at a time until at least half the oil has been beaten in, then incorporate the rest in large amounts.

Serve some or all of the following, cooked and at room temperature. If you are selecting only a few, be sure to pick foods that contrast in shape, texture, and color: salt cod, boiled beef, artichokes (one for each person), chickpeas, cauliflower (separated into flowerets), small boiled potatoes in their skins, hard-boiled egg halves, quartered tomatoes, green beans.

⋙ HUNGARIAN CHICKEN

A dish that is better made ahead a day or so and reheated.

¼ lb. butter
1 cup onions, chopped
2 2½-lb. chickens, cut up
salt
cayenne pepper, to taste
2 tablespoons flour
1 pint sour cream

Sauté the onions in butter. Transfer to the bottom of a deep casserole that has a tightly fitting lid. Lightly sprinkle the uncooked pieces of chicken with salt and cayenne. (Be generous but not reckless with this seasoning, for tolerances will vary. Start with a small amount, say ¼ teaspoon for the two chickens, and increase the amount each time until you have found the amount that is perfect for you.) Arrange in the casserole on the bed of onions with the heaviest pieces of chicken on the bottom and the smallest and lightest pieces on the top. Cover tightly and let the chickens stew in their own juices for 45 to 60 minutes in a 350° oven. Baste occasionally with a baster, being careful to replace the lid. Sprinkle the flour over the chicken and add the sour cream. Put in the oven for 10 minutes more and serve. Serves 8.

Serve with Armenian pilaf*; orange, grapefruit, and tangerine segments on a bed of greens with a tart dressing (2 parts olive oil, 1 part grapefruit juice, 1 teaspoon grated lemon rind, salt, pepper); Vienna bread; coffee granita*.

ᵛₛ GULYAS

Gulyas is a vastly superior stew subtly seasoned with two kinds of paprika and other spices and cooked with a surprising amount of onions. The paprikas must be from Hungary; nondescript red dust labeled paprika just will not do. If the hot paprika is not available, use all sweet paprika. This is a superb party dish, pleasing to the guests and easy on the host or hostess, since its flavor is greatly improved by reheating.

3 lbs. onions, chopped
¾ cup oil, more if necessary
1 tablespoon sharp or hot paprika
1 tablespoon sweet Hungarian paprika
(or 3 tablespoons if hot paprika is not available)
3 lbs. beef chuck, cut into 2½-inch chunks
1 clove garlic, smashed or minced
all the peel cut very thin from 1 lemon
1 tablespoon caraway seeds, mashed in mortar
1 bay leaf
1 sprig fresh rosemary or 1 teaspoon dried
salt
beef stock, if necessary

Sauté the onions in the oil until translucent. Sprinkle with the hot and sweet paprikas. Continue stirring until golden. Transfer with a slotted spoon to a heavy casserole. Brown the meat on all sides in the same pan as the onions, adding more oil if necessary. Add the meat and oil from the pan to the casserole along with the garlic, the *thin* lemon peel, caraway seeds, bay leaf, rosemary, and salt. Cover and simmer for a long time (several hours at least). Add some beef stock if the meat starts to get too dry. If the heat is low enough, the onions will provide enough moisture. Leave overnight and reheat before serving. Serves 4 to 6.

Serve with dill pickle; steamed potatoes or spaetzle*; watercress; espresso and liqueurs.

ᴥᵹ SZEKELY GULYAS

Sauerkraut had no particular lure for me until I tried this dish at the urging of a Czechoslovakian friend. It has other names, but the results are essentially the same—sauerkraut at its most sublime. It is another of the dishes that is even better the second day or made ahead.

¾ *cup diced onions*
3 tablespoons fat, preferably bacon
1 lb. veal, cut into 1½-inch cubes
1 lb. pork, cut into 1½-inch cubes
flour
2 tablespoons sweet Hungarian paprika
(no colored dust from the supermarket)
2 lbs. sauerkraut, preferably in bulk (not canned)
2 tablespoons caraway seeds (not obligatory)
salt, pepper
1 pint sour cream

Cook the onions in the fat until limp and translucent. Meanwhile dust the veal and pork cubes lightly with the flour. Sauté in the pan with the onions until brown on all sides. Add the paprika and stir around. Rinse the sauerkraut and squeeze the moisture out. (This is not necessary if you like the flavor very sour.) Stir into the meat and onions. Cover and cook slowly until the meat is tender. Add the caraway seeds, if you like them, salt and pepper, and stir in the sour cream. Heat slightly; do *not* let it boil. Serves 4 to 6.

Serve with sliced cucumbers with vinaigrette dressing seasoned with tarragon; Marlborough apple pie*.

⋐⋛ SIAMESE CURRY

In Thailand curry is used in the Asian way, with handfuls of this and that seasoning tossed into the food, as the mood moves the cook. It is somewhat startling to see seasonings measured by fractions of a cup rather than by teaspoons and tablespoons, but the curries always taste good and sometimes better after reheating, so that this quantity for 8 could serve 4 people for two days.

> *4 lbs. cubed beef and pork (a little more beef than pork)*
> *3–4 onions, chopped*
> *3–4 cloves garlic, minced*
> *⅓ cup cooking oil or fat from the meat*
> *⅓ cup coriander seeds*
> *⅓ cup ground cumin*
> *1 tablespoon Bovril (beef concentrate)*
> *⅔ can evaporated milk*
> *1 tablespoon anchovy paste (this is a satisfactory substitute*
> *for the fermented fish paste used in Siam)*
> *grated rind of ½ lemon*
> *black and red pepper to taste*
> *2–3 cups milk or dry skimmed milk, diluted*
> *3½ oz. grated coconut*
> *⅓ cup chopped mint leaves*

Sear the beef and pork in a skillet and transfer to a bowl. Sauté the onion and garlic in enough cooking oil or fat from the meat to cover the bottom of the skillet. Rub the coriander and cumin between your palms, letting the heat of your hands warm it a bit. Add it to the onions and garlic and cook it a bit in the fat. Add the Bovril and the evaporated milk, anchovy paste, lemon rind, and black and red pepper. Let it simmer awhile, adding the milk as it starts to dry out. Add the meat cubes and coconut and simmer, covered, for 1 to 2 hours, or more. About half an hour before serving, add the mint leaves. Serves 8.

Serve with rice; fresh, frozen, or canned toasted grated coconut; chopped peanuts; French-fried onion rings; diced fried bananas; sweet-and-sour cucumbers (diced cucumbers soaked in sweetened vinegar); chutney or watermelon pickle.

◄§ MARYLAND STUFFED HAM

This is traditionally served at Eastertime in St. Mary's County, Maryland. The greens that are used as stuffing vary from cook to cook. The idea of adding them to the ham is said to come from the days when Lenten fasting was more serious than it is now, for they "diluted" the shock of the fatty ham for bodies that had been fasting severely. Year-old country hams were mostly used, because the older ones were too hard to stuff. In those days of course cooks had had no contact with the pallid mockeries labeled ham in most food stores these days. This adaptation, therefore, is best made with a Dutch, Danish, or Polish canned ham.

> *2 lbs. fresh spinach, chopped*
> *3–4 scallions, finely chopped*
> *½ cup chopped mint leaves*
> *1 teaspoon red pepper, or crumbled dried red pods*
> *salt, if necessary*
> *1 canned ham, 3–5 lbs.*

Mix the spinach, scallions, mint leaves, red pepper, and just a speck of salt. (The imported canned hams are usually not as salty as most uncooked hams but use some caution.)   Put in a sieve and dip into boiling water for a few seconds and drain immediately, pressing excess moisture out with paper towels.   Poke holes here and there around the sides of the ham with a knife or carving steel.   Push the spinach mixture inside the holes.   The old cooking method was to sew the country ham in cheese cloth and boil.   The new way is to wrap it in aluminum foil and bake for an hour or two at 350°. The hams are pre-cooked, but this helps the flavors to permeate the ham.   Serve at room temperature.   A 3-lb. ham will serve 6 to 8.

Serve with spoon bread*; asparagus vinaigrette; chocolate mousse*.

⋐§ CALABACITAS CON CHILE VERDE (SUMMER SQUASH AND GREEN CHILI)

This pale and lovely combination of colors is eaten with great delight by those served it for the first time and with ever greater bliss by its devotees.   Some versions add a cup of fresh corn cut from the cob, but why tamper with near perfection?

1 clove garlic, minced
½ small onion, chopped
3 tablespoons butter
4 medium yellow summer squash, diced but not peeled
½ cup milk
½ cup (4-oz.) chopped canned green chilies
¾ cup diced or grated Monterey Jack,
mild Cheddar, or mozzarella cheese
salt

Sauté the garlic and onion briefly in the butter.   Remove with a slotted spoon and reserve.   Cook the squash (which may also be zucchini) in the same butter until slightly translucent.   Turn into a shallow casserole and sprinkle with the onion and garlic.   Add the milk.   Strew the chilies and cheese over the squash.   Sprinkle lightly with salt. Bake in a preheated 350° oven for 25 to 30 minutes or until the cheese is melted and the squash is tender. Serves 4.

Serve with thick broiled hamburgers; Italian bread; ice cream.

❧ CURRIED FRUIT CASSEROLE

An amiable dish whether served with a roast turkey and crisp watercress salad or as a piquant finish to a simple meal, say of pasta and pesto.

4 cups mixed fruit, such as:
1 cup dried apricots, soaked 1 or 2 hours in water
2 oranges, peeled, seeded, sliced thin
1 8-oz. can pear halves
1 9-oz. can dark sweet cherries, drained
½ cup butter
1 tablespoon curry powder
about ⅔ cup brown sugar

Drain fruit and arrange in a shallow casserole. Melt the butter with the curry powder and pour over the fruit. Sprinkle with brown sugar. The amount of sugar will vary according to the sweetness of the fruit used. Bake uncovered in a preheated 325° oven for 45 minutes. Remove from the oven and let stand for at least 2 hours to let the flavors ripen. Reheat for 15 minutes before serving. Serves 4 to 6.

Serve with roast pork; baked kasha*; French crêpes rolled around sweetened whipped cream flavored with Cointreau and topped with chocolate sauce.

❧ FROZEN PRESERVED GINGER
IN WHIPPED CREAM

Although I care about all spices, I find ginger the most exciting and inspiriting. Green, or fresh, ginger used to be found only in the Chinese areas in big cities, but now, thanks to the proliferation of specialty foods and seasonings, it may be found often in suburban supermarkets. The roots (rhizomes) are light tan with a somewhat wrinkled skin and have a sharp and pungent flavor. Usually for aesthetic reasons they are peeled, then chopped fine before being used in cooking. Green ginger is used with verve and special understanding by the Chinese, the Indians, and the English. Other cuisines don't explore the fascinating ways to use green ginger, although most do use the powdered form in baking. The best of the powdered varieties is from Jamaica and has a long shelf life, often becoming sharper when it is a year or two old.

To one who truly cares about ginger, this simple and inspired combination is a delectable ending to a meal. And it doesn't matter whether it's frozen or not; it is equally fine simply chilled.

½ cup preserved ginger and syrup, or just ginger syrup
2 cups heavy cream, lightly whipped

Chop the ginger fine and mix the ginger and syrup with the cream. Chill in the refrigerator or put in the freezer until frozen. If you choose the latter method, remove the dish from the freezer 30 minutes before serving. Serves 8 richly.

Serve after Turkish pilaf*; orange and black-olive salad*.

A Liveliness of Shellfish

I have had a long and joyous love affair with all the beautiful shellfish I have encountered during my peripatetic and unmossy life. I have eaten lobsters in Canada, Maine, and on Cape Cod; river shrimp in Charleston and at a beautiful mountaintop hotel in Puerto Rico, and all kinds of shrimp in New Orleans; hard- and soft-shell clams up and down the East Coast; crabs that were in the Chesapeake only *minutes* before cooking; stone crabs in Florida from nearby waters; and oysters native to wherever I have been. All are sublime when eaten at their place of origin, but now they are in markets all over the country, arriving by plane, boat, and train, fresh, frozen and canned—not only from both our oceans and the Gulf of Mexico but from all the waters of the earth—in large amounts and exciting varieties.

Shellfish are always a delight to their admirers. They need only brief cooking and, except for such wantonly rich dishes as lobster thermidor, are low in calories, and there is little or no waste. The only real drawbacks are in coping with lively, vigorous crabs and lobsters and with the allergies that a few people have to some shellfish.

Eating a lobster properly is often a puzzling procedure at first, but it can be simple and fun once you know how. Twist off the claws of the boiled lobster and crack each claw with a lobster cracker, or with a sturdy nutcracker, or a wooden mallet, like those used for crabs in Maryland and Virginia. (The eager and ingenious have even been known to use rocks and hammers.) Separate the tail from the body by bending it back until it cracks. Break the flippers off the tail and discard. Begin to eat with a fork where the flippers broke off, dipping each piece in melted butter first. Unhinge the back from the body, and discard the back. The tomalley, or liver, found in the body turns a lovely yellowish green when cooked and is considered by many to be the best part of the lobster. Open the

186

body of the lobster by cracking it apart sideways with both hands. There is some good meat there. Aficionados put the small wispy claws in their mouth and daintily suck the meat out as if they were using a straw. In many American restaurants specializing in sea-food, you are given a large bib, but this is not really necessary. Lobster has to be messy if it's to be thoroughly enjoyed. Where decorum is important, lobster is served in a different way. At formal dinners or in fancy restaurants it is presented in a more accessible guise, or the waiter is instructed to do all the work for you.

⤳ CLAM CURRY CUSTARD

An unstereotyped pleasure with cocktails or a preprandial wine.

5 eggs
¾ teaspoon salt
1½ teaspoons curry powder
1 tablespoon sherry
¾ cup minced clams
toast pieces

Put the eggs, salt, curry powder, sherry, and 1½ cups water in an electric blender. Blend for 15 seconds. Remove, add the clams, and stir in. Pour into two buttered 9-inch quiche pans or pie tins. Put in larger pans of hot water. Bake in a 325° oven for 25 to 30 minutes, or until a knife inserted comes out clean. Cut into diamonds, squares, or other shapes. Serve warm on pieces of toast cut into the same shapes. Makes 25 to 50 pieces, depending on size.

Serve with broiled chicken breasts; puréed green beans; noodles with butter and poppy seeds; lemon angel food cake.

⤳ CRAB FEAST

This is not a dainty meal, nor one for the timid cook. It is best eaten out of doors on rustic tables with plenty of paper napkins. Some directions blandly assume that live crabs lie quietly awaiting their fate like oysters or clams while the preliminary preparations are going on. In reality, they aren't in the least passive, and caution must be taken in handling them. I speak with feeling, remembering some extra violent and aggressive crabs that got under the stove. I did win, finally. I was bigger.

vinegar
4 dozen live hard-shell or blue crabs
Old Bay sea-food seasoning (or crab boil)
salt
butter

Take your largest cooking pot and place folded wire mesh, a trivet, or some other easily penetrable stand in it, so that the crabs will rest about 2 inches above the bottom of the pot. The crabs must be steamed and should not touch the boiling liquid below them. Mix 1 part vinegar to 2 parts water, enough to cover the bottom of the pot to a depth of about 1 inch. Bring this to a boil. To handle crabs, use kitchen tongs of some sort, and pick them up one at a time. Check each one to make sure that it is still alive—there are sometimes one or two fatalities per batch. Using a large spoon, sprinkle a generous amount of Old Bay seasoning on the underside of each crab as you pick it up, then a generous amount of salt. This will irritate the crab and make it move violently, but deposit it firmly on the rack in the pot. Place as many crabs in the pot as it will hold with the lid fit tightly. If you are using a smallish pot, you will have to steam them in several shifts. Keep using the same steaming mixture but add a little more water and vinegar if needed. Cover and steam for 15 to 20 minutes. When they are done, place the crabs on strips of paper toweling or newspaper to drain and cool. Melt the butter and pour ½ cup into small dishes, one for each person.

To eat the crabs, open the flap on the underside and use it as a lever to lift the top shell off. Remove all the insides that are not covered by a thin shell. Break the crab in half and then, with a knife or your fingers, section the sides of the crab, one section to each leg. Remove the surrounding shell to get the white meat within. The claw meat is obtained by breaking the claw open with a wooden mallet. Dip the meat in melted butter. Serves 8.

Serve with Maryland crab soup*; watermelon; beer.

✒️ MARYLAND CRAB SOUP

In Maryland the soup that precedes an orgy of steamed hard-shell crabs is somewhat of an orgy itself, not a dainty prelude to a meal. In the soup there are crabs, of course. If you are near to the source, the whole crab is put into the soup, which has a base of chicken or beef (beef is the favorite) and bacon and some of all the fresh vegetables you can find at crab time around the Chesapeake. If you are making this where there is no supply of fresh crab, canned or frozen may be used, with frozen cracked Dungeness crab claws put in to add an authentic clutter. This is not the kind of dish that you whip up for a few. It is made when there are going to be 10 to 12. A streamlined version may be made by starting with a large bag of frozen mixed vegetables, plus some canned tomatoes, potatoes, onions, and cabbage, a few bouillon cubes or beef stew meat, and, naturally, crabs.

6 steamed crabs (see preceding recipe),
or 1 lb. canned or frozen
1 lb. shin beef, in one piece
¼ lb. bacon, unsliced
3 tomatoes, quartered
3 potatoes, peeled and diced
1 onion, chopped
1 cup whole-kernel corn, cut from the cob
or frozen or canned
1 cup lima beans
1 cup string beans, cut in pieces
2 stalks celery, diced
2 carrots, diced
1 cup finely shredded cabbage
¼ cup chopped parsley
¾ cup beer
4 quarts water
1 teaspoon mustard
4 tablespoons butter or margarine
2 teaspoons seafood seasoning or Worcestershire sauce

Break off claws from bodies of crabs, discard small ones, and crack large ones. Pull off back shell, remove gills or devil and face of crab (eyes and sandbag should come off with shell). Break crab in half and cut across each half, parallel to shells, but do not remove meat. Combine these body pieces, large claws, beef, bacon, vegetables, beer, water, mustard, butter, and seasoning. Simmer 1 to 2 hours. French bread and beer accompany it. Serves 10 to 12.

✺§ CRAB NORFOLK

This is the way to enjoy fresh lump crab meat at its blissful best, and I'm afraid it would not taste at all the same made from frozen or canned crab. Served sizzling hot, it is surprisingly filling; few but the most rugged and stalwart eaters can eat much else. Sliced tomatoes are traditionally served in individual salad bowls with crab Norfolk. I like to sprinkle them with finely chopped basil.

1 lb. lump or backfin crab meat
½ cup (1 stick) butter
1 tablespoon vinegar or lemon juice
salt
shake of red cayenne pepper

Pick over the crab meat and remove any membranes, but do not pull it to pieces. Divide into four shallow individual casseroles, preferably metal ones. Melt the butter and mix with vinegar or lemon juice and the seasonings. Pour over crab meat and heat briefly in the oven or under a broiler until sizzling. Rush to the table. Serves 4.

Serve with sliced tomatoes sprinkled with finely chopped basil; salt sticks; tangerine sherbet.

CRAB SALAD

It seems a little cruel and tantalizing to say, as I have, in several recipes, that you really must have lump crab meat, when it is available at a decent price only in certain sections along the Eastern seaboard. Crab salad may, of course, be made with canned or frozen crab meat.

1½ lbs. lump or backfin crab meat
or 3 cans (6½-oz.) crab meat
or 3 packages frozen king crab meat
½ cup chopped celery
¾ cup mayonnaise (not "salad dressing")
garden lettuce
yellow plum or cherry tomatoes
1 tablespoon capers

Remove any membranes from the crab meat, but do not pull it to pieces. Toss lightly with celery and mayonnaise. Chill. To serve, bed the crabmeat down on garden lettuce, surround with tomatoes, and sprinkle the top with capers. Serves 4 to 6.

Serve with sliced country ham; hot biscuits; blackberry pie.

AVOCADO WITH CRAB SALAD

Avocado halves and crab salad (or indeed shrimp or chicken salad) are a perfect combination, being delicate but surprisingly filling. This is perhaps my favorite of all main-dish salads.

½ lb. lump crab meat, picked and membranes removed,
or ½ lb. cooked shrimp, peeled and deveined,
or 2 cups cooked, diced chicken
(see recipe for poached chicken*)
¼ cup mayonnaise, preferably homemade
2 tablespoons chopped celery
2 ripe avocados, cut in half and stored but not peeled

Mix the crab meat with mayonnaise and celery and pile into avocado halves. Serves 4.

✎§ CRAB CAKES

In earlier days around the Chesapeake before pizza became ubiquitous, crab cakes were a favorite snack or the star of a meal. I never have had a poor one, though some are better than others. Some people use backfin crab meat, some use regular, and some use the dark meat from the claws. Each kind of crab meat has its adherents. Most agree that, like pie dough, the less the crab meat is handled, the tenderer the cake. I prefer lump crab meat barely mixed, and no breadcrumbs added.

1 lb. crab meat
2 tablespoons mayonnaise
1 tablespoon prepared mustard
1 teaspoon finely chopped parsley
¼ teaspoon salt
1 large egg
butter
oil

Pick over the crab meat, removing the membranes, but handling it as little as possible. Mix all the other ingredients except the butter and oil together in a small bowl. Add the crab meat and barely mix, using a spoon and not your hands. Make into cakes about 2½ inches in diameter, again handling as little as possible. The cakes should be rather flat. Sauté in a mixture of butter and oil about ½ inch deep. Makes 8 to 9 crab cakes.

Serve with baked corn custard*, cole slaw, French bread; watermelon.

✑ UNCOMMON LOBSTER COCKTAIL

Once when I was visiting on Cape Cod, I was astonished to find no instructions in all the cookbooks in the house for cooking a lobster over two pounds. We had been lucky enough to find a six pounder, and we had to call the fishman. A lobster this size is tender and juicy when steamed for 35 minutes, and you will get about 5½ cups of meat. That is usually enough for one main dish and a lobster cocktail for another meal or to fill avocado halves when mixed with chopped celery and mayonnaise. When cooked, it will keep several days or a week in the refrigerator, and several weeks if frozen.

½ cup unsalted butter, softened to room temperature
2 tablespoons finely chopped fresh dill or fresh tarragon
2 tablespoons fresh lemon juice
salt, pepper
2 cups diced cooked meat

Beat butter until fluffy. Add fresh chopped dill or tarragon, if available. If not, use chives or parsley. Add lemon juice, salt and pepper to taste, and cream some more. Chill before serving. Makes about ¼ cup of sauce to be served with the cold lobster.

Serve with succotash; Bibb lettuce; red plum halves and honeydew melon balls in white wine with curaçao.

✑ LOBSTER STEW

There is something poetic about the flavor and simplicity of lobster stew, and one of the best recipes comes from the poet Robert P. Tristram Coffin. He felt as strongly about the good foods from Maine as he did about poetry. This stew should be made of the very best ingredients, and the best, to him, were good Maine lobsters, whole milk, and cream. The flavors must be allowed to ripen in a cold place or refrigerator for a day or two before the stew is reheated and served. This recipe may be doubled or tripled without disturb-ing the proportions.

4 small-to-medium live lobsters
½ cup boiling sea water or ½ cup boiling water
with a teaspoon of salt added
¼ lb. slightly salted butter
1 quart whole milk, scalded
2 cups light cream, scalded
salt, pepper

Pick up the lobsters from the back with tongs, or if you're really brave, with your hands, and drop them into a huge pot full of rap-idly boiling water. Cover the pot and steam for 10 minutes over a high heat. Drain the lobsters, let them cool, and shell, removing the meat as neatly as possible. Discard the intestinal vein and lungs. Melt the butter in a large pot and add the lobster meat, which you have cut into pieces. Remove from the heat and slowly add, stirring constantly, the scalded milk and cream. Add salt and pepper. Sim-mer for a few minutes, but do not boil. Remove from heat and cool for at least 24 to 48 hours while the flavor is developing. Dr. Coffin did not believe in refrigeration, but he lived in Maine where it is cool enough to keep this stew for two days without spoiling. Farther south I would definitely keep this in the refrigerator. Re-heat before serving and season to taste. Serves 4.

Serve with broiled chestnuts wrapped in bacon; dill pickles; Pilot crackers; homemade doughnuts.

ᐤᔲ MUSSELS STEAMED IN WINE

One of my favorite of all shellfish dishes and one of the simplest —uncluttered except for the beautiful, gleaming black shells with their pearly insides, so handsome with the pale orange-colored flesh.

¼ cup olive oil
2 chopped scallions

2 tablespoons chopped parsley, preferably the flat-leaf kind
2 finely minced garlic cloves
1 teaspoon oregano
pinch of pepper
1 cup dry white wine
5 lbs. mussels in their shells, well scrubbed

Put all the ingredients except the mussels in a soup pan. Bring to a boil. Add the mussels, cover, and turn the heat down to low. The mussels take about 5 to 10 minutes to open and are a pretty orange. Tear off one shell from each, but leave the rest in the juices. Use the shells for scooping up liquid; an oyster fork is usual for eating the mussels. Divide among 6 large, warm soup bowls. Serve with French bread to mop up the juices.

Serve with mixed green salad; apricot tarts.

⋖ HAM AND OYSTER PIE

A delicate, festive, and yet filling dish, for a late breakfast or a light supper. As is to be expected, the choicer the ham and the fresher the oysters, the better the dish. Any pastry top may be used, but the cream-cheese pastry is special.

1 lb. baking ham, diced
2 tablespoons butter
2 tablespoons flour
½ cup milk
½ cup white wine
oyster liquor
salt, pepper
1 pint fresh, or 2 packages frozen, oysters
1½ lbs. fresh peas, shelled, or 1 10-oz. package frozen peas
cream-cheese pastry for 1 crust (see recipe for coulibiac*)

Simmer the ham in water to cover for 15 minutes while you make the cream sauce. Melt the butter in a saucepan and blend in the flour, stirring for a minute or two. Add the liquids, including the juice from the oysters (there should be 1½ cups in all), and the seasonings. Cook, stirring constantly until the sauce is smooth and thick. Drain the ham and add the oysters and peas. Stir into cream sauce and pour into a low buttered casserole. Fit the pastry on top, crimping the edges. Slash the top, to allow steam to escape. Bake 30 minutes in a 350° oven. Serves 4.

Serve with romaine salad with vinaigrette dressing; buttermilk biscuits.

◆§ SCALLOPS WITH BUTTER AND VERMOUTH

Scallops with their wonderfully subtle flavor and texture are best when cooked very simply and briefly.

½ stick (⅛ lb.) butter
1½ lbs. scallops, preferably small bay scallops
¼ cup dry vermouth or dry white wine

Melt the butter. Sauté the scallops for 2 to 3 minutes, or until they are opaque—no longer. Add the vermouth and keep it over the heat just long enough to get it warm. Serve immediately. No other seasoning is needed. Serves 4.

Serve with spaetzle* with pesto*; raw mushroom salad*, coffee tortoni*.

◆§ COQUILLES SAINT-JACQUES

The delicate meat of scallops needs brief cooking and subtle seasoning. One of the best ways to serve it is in this classic dish, which is usually served in individual baking shells. These can be found in most houseware departments or shops specializing in classic cooking equipment.

1 lb. sea or bay scallops
¼ cup (½ stick) butter

1 shallot, finely chopped, or 1 small white onion, chopped
¼ lb. sliced fresh mushrooms
¼ teaspoon pepper (no salt)
¼ cup dry white wine
breadcrumbs
more butter

Cut the scallops in quarters, if the large ones; in thirds for the small ones. Simmer in the butter with the shallot or onion and the mushrooms 2 to 3 minutes over medium heat. Add pepper and wine and cook only a minute or two. Put in the scallop shells or a small casserole and sprinkle the top with breadcrumbs. Dot with butter and bake in 500° oven for 3 minutes. Serve immediately. Serves 4.

Serve with rice cooked in chicken broth with white raisins and a lump of butter; marinated cooked leeks and celery; hot party rolls.

⪜ SHRIMP MOUSSE WITH WHITE GRAPES AND WATERCRESS

This is a beautiful dish for a luncheon, a buffet, or even a wedding at home. There is no need for a dressing; it's in the mousse.

2 envelopes unflavored gelatin
¼ cup dry vermouth
½ cup hot orange juice, or ½ cup hot chicken broth
2 tablespoons lemon juice
¼ cup mayonnaise
1 cup sour cream
1 tablespoon finely chopped fresh dill
or 1 teaspoon dill mixture or ½ teaspoon dill seed
salt, pepper
1 lb. cooked shrimp, peeled and deveined,
or 2 5-oz. cans shrimp, rinsed and drained
1 cup white grapes
watercress

Put the gelatin in the container of an electric blender with the vermouth, hot orange juice or hot chicken broth, and lemon juice. Cover and blend for about 10 seconds. Add the mayonnaise, sour cream, seasonings, and about half the shrimp. Blend for 1 or 2 minutes, add the rest of the shrimp, and blend until smooth. Remove from blender, stir in white grapes, and turn into a 5-cup mold that has been first rinsed in cold water. Chill until firm. Unmold and surround with watercress and whole shrimp, if desired.

This dish may be made without a blender if the shrimp are mashed or put through a food mill or a meat grinder, using the finest blades. Soak the gelatin in ¼ cup cold water and then dissolve in vermouth, hot orange juice or chicken broth, and lemon juice. Mix with the ground shrimp, mayonnaise, and sour cream and follow the rest of the directions above. Serves 4.

Serve with hot barley and mushroom casserole; hot rolls; Paris-Brest*.

❧ SHRIMP PASTE

There is no reason at all to ever buy those nondescript fish pastes sold in glass jars or cans when this superior paste can be made so easily. I have even made it with frozen cooked or canned shrimp in emergency, and it was still better than the commercial variety.

½ lb. uncooked shrimp, peeled and deveined
2 tablespoons unsalted butter plus ¼ cup (½ stick) butter,
softened but not melted
1 teaspoon grated lemon rind
3 tablespoons sherry or dry vermouth

Cook the shrimp in the 2 tablespoons of butter until barely opaque and colored. Remove from heat. Mash with a fork and mix well with the rest of the butter and other ingredients. Pack into a pottery crock and chill until needed.

Serve with melba toast or good crackers with cocktails.

✒ SHRIMP WITH FETA CHEESE

Shrimp with tomatoes and feta cheese, with or without dill, is an especially captivating combination of flavors. Luckily, feta may be found in more and more places around the country, in cheese stores and even some supermarkets, for there is no exact equivalent for its beguiling saltiness and sharpness, with its surprising dead-white color. Naturally the Greeks are apt to start with their wonderful sun-ripened tomatoes. New York's tomatoes for the most part are cottony and colorless, so one must make some compromises at least in this area.

⅓ cup chopped onions
3 tablespoons olive oil
1 plump clove garlic, minced
2 cups fresh, good skinned and diced tomatoes,
or 3 cups canned Italian plum tomatoes cooked down to 2 cups
½ cup dry white wine or dry vermouth
½ cup chopped parsley, preferably the flat Italian type
1½ lbs. peeled uncooked shrimp
¼ lb. feta cheese, crumbled

Cook the onions in the olive oil until translucent. Add the garlic and tomatoes, either the fresh or cooked-down canned ones. Add the wine and parsley and simmer, adding more wine or water if the sauce gets too thick. Add the shrimp and crumbled cheese. (This can be done ahead of time.) Cook the mixture on top of the stove or bake in a preheated 350° oven until the shrimp are pink and the cheese is melted. Serves 4.

Serve with watercress and arugula salad with vinaigrette dressing; pideh*; lemon granita*.

◈ SEAFOOD CASSEROLE

Simply and serenely satisfying.

½ lb. scallops
½ lb. fresh mushrooms, sliced
½ lb. raw shrimp, peeled and deveined
¼ cup butter
½ cup heavy cream
2 tablespoons sherry or brandy
2 tablespoons finely chopped chives or parsley
salt, pepper
breadcrumbs
more butter

Sauté the scallops, mushrooms, and shrimp in the butter until barely cooked. Put in a casserole with the juices and butter from the pan. Add the cream, sherry or brandy, chives or parsley, salt, and pepper. Sprinkle the top with breadcrumbs. Dot with more butter and put in a 350° oven for 20 to 25 minutes. Serves 4 to 6.

Serve with purée of peas; glazed oranges*.

A Nourishment of Soups and Stews

Soup is one of the most ancient dishes in the world, as much the essence of life as bread and wine. As Bishop Latour says in Willa Cather's *Death Comes for the Archbishop*, after tasting one of Father Vaillant's soups, "A soup like this is not the work of one man. It is the result of a constantly refined tradition. There are nearly a thousand years of history in this soup." That particular soup of Father Vaillant's was a rich, dark, and suave onion soup. The combination of ingredients was not quite that old, but Bishop Latour was obviously thinking back to the first man who grew an onion and put it into a pot with meat and water to make a broth.

Soup is one of the most comforting dishes to make, pleasurable in its aroma and in the companionable sound of its quiet burbling. On a long gray day when all is not right with my world, a pot of soup simmering on the stove soothes and heartens me in an undemanding way. In the making it nourishes my spirits much as it nourishes and sustains me physically later on.

To make soup one needs good ingredients but not expensive ones. It is also a good idea to have some skill, some intelligence, and the good sense to leave well enough alone—to omit superfluities. A cook with good instincts and a gay imagination can make the same soup yet never repeat it from one year to the next.

These days with supermarkets everywhere in the land, few people have a butcher, much less someone to save them free soupbones. However, an interested and determined bone collector can find some from time to time in the meat sections of the supermarket tidily packaged and labeled. It is best to buy lots and squirrel them away in the freezer against the time you will want them. A soup-making day or mood may come upon one suddenly, and if a suitable number of ingredients are on hand, one can satisfy it and enjoy it.

Even in a city apartment it is possible to keep some bones in the freezer, and some onions, carrots, lemons, celery, potatoes, and herbs elsewhere. Canned tomatoes, beef or chicken stock (homemade or canned), barley, all kinds of beans (canned or dried), rice, pasta in various small, charming shapes (wagon wheels, butterflies, seashells, and so forth), and some of those prettily layered packages of legumes, barley, and seasonings called minestrone mix are all useful soup staples. And one or two frozen green vegetables can always be called into service during the last minutes of cooking for a fresh, crisp accent.

A veteran soup maker feels particularly good when there is a ham bone in the refrigerator or the carcass of a roast chicken, duck, or turkey, as well as some compatible cooked vegetables and cooked meats. However, a soup pot is not a disposal pot. Some things do not taste good together, so be sure to select with caution, imagination, and taste. Discard the mediocre and unharmonious.

Sometimes a soup will be all right but may taste a little flat. When that happens, try one or two of the following (but not all) to make the flavor sparkle: a lemon, sliced thin; a few seeded, peeled tomatoes or tomato paste or purée; coarse salt (just a few crystals); a chopped onion, sautéed or raw; a dash of an herb, powdered first in the palm of the hand; some chopped fresh dill (one of the best soup herbs, with an interesting flavor *and* fragrance); a little grated cheese; or a dollop of sour cream.

After a soup has been made and served, refrigerate or freeze any that remains. Those dreamy instructions in old books about keeping the soup on the back of the stove and reheating once a day do not make sense these days. It is true that houses used to be kept colder, but people in those days must have been less affected by the sneaky bacilli in spoiled food or else they blamed stomachaches on something else. Soups that are left out of the refrigerator will sometimes ferment overnight or, if left longer, can grow a rich and repulsive-looking fungus. Soup can get a tired taste and appearance after too much reheating, so it is best to freeze it in small containers and use only what you need each time, adding one of the flavor sparklers described above, a package of frozen green vegetables, or a dash of wine. Freezing is especially fine for a household of one or two people because it is possible to have the pleasure of making and eating soup without the boredom of eating it night after night until it is gone. Also it is a nice secure feeling to have some stashed away in the freezer.

Some special equipment is needed for soup making but not much. A two- or three-gallon pot is necessary for the bulky stages of making stock or minestrone or other large soups. In the first lean but happy years of our marriage, my husband and I bought a beautiful antique Russian copper soup pot that has been part of every kitchen I have had since then. Your pot can be of inexpensive enamelware, heavy cast aluminum, stainless steel, copper, or what you will. A cast-iron Dutch oven will do for some soups but will turn those with tomatoes an undecorative dark color. If the soup pot has a long handle, it can hang on the wall out of the way and can be used to steam lobsters or crabs or mussels, cook pasta, and other foods requiring a large pan. A colander and a food mill or an electric blender will be needed to drain and purée soups. Most kitchens have sharp knives for chopping, long wooden spoons for stirring, a bulb baster for removing fat from the top of a soup when there is not time to chill it, and plastic containers for storing the results.

Soup is a hospitable dish, adaptable to the complexities of present-day living when children come and go on incompatible schedules, to lazy Sunday nights when the hour for eating depends upon the mood, to the currently chic and relaxed kind of entertainment when people come for cocktails and stay for soup and leisurely conversation.

Cooking times given in this chapter are approximate. Even in these days of controlled temperatures, each stove has its own idiosyncrasies, and the age and tenderness of meat and vegetables may vary considerably. Most soups, except for a few cream soups, can manage varying heats, although low or medium is usually the best.

✒ BOURRIDE

To my mind this French dish is the best of all fish soups, deceptively bland and unexpectedly filling. Its creamy texture makes it

seem appropriate as a delicate prelude to a meal, but with bread, vegetables, and salad, it is a meal for all but the most hearty eaters.

2 lbs. any kind of fresh fish, cut in pieces
1 carrot, chopped
1 onion, chopped
1 stalk celery, chopped
1 sprig parsley, minced
1 bay leaf
6–8 peppercorns
some mushroom peelings
¼ cup white wine or 2 tablespoons vinegar
1 cup aioli*
1 cup bread cubes, fried in butter

Trim and bone the fish. Prepare a court bouillon by simmering
the remaining ingredients except the aioli and bread in one quart of
water for 30 minutes. Strain the bouillon and poach the fish in the
liquid very gently for about 10 minutes, or until the fish is opaque
and flakes easily with a fork. Remove half the fish and mash the
rest in the broth to get as much of the essence as possible. Strain
and let the liquid cool slightly. Put the aioli in the top of a double
boiler and add the warm fish broth bit by bit, stirring until it is
creamy and thick. Do not allow it to boil. Serve in bowls with a
few pieces of fish and a few bread cubes in each. Serves 4.

Serve with crisp French-fried eggplant*; green salad, French bread.

ᵊᔓ CARROT SOUP

This beautiful buttery soup looks as if marigold petals were floating
in it, but it tastes better. It is only as good as the carrots with which
it is made, however. Young carrots are best; older carrots should
have their woody centers cut out and discarded. The soup can be
made with chicken or veal stock, but it is perfectly good made with

plain water. Bouillon cubes are to be avoided in any case. I have used rice here as a thickener, but a diced medium potato will do as well; I just think the rice is a little prettier.

2 cups sliced peeled young carrots
½ cup coarsely chopped onions
1 tablespoon sugar
¼ cup melted butter
1 tablespoon lemon juice
salt, pepper
½ cup raw rice
4 cups chicken stock or veal stock or water
Garnish: very finely chopped parsley or fresh dill or diced pimiento

Put the carrots in a blender with the onion, sugar, melted butter, lemon juice, salt, and pepper until coarsely chopped, stopping the blender and stirring several times with a rubber scraper. Turn into a heavy-bottomed pan and simmer for 15 to 20 minutes, or until the raw taste is gone from the carrots. Add the rice and the stock or water, and simmer until the rice is tender. Serves 4 to 6.

Serve with yellow tomato, scallion, and black walnut salad*; coffee granita*.

◆§ RUMANIAN CIORBA WITH MEATBALLS

The national soup of Rumania is ciorba, which may be made with almost any kind of meat or fish, and even with vegetables alone. It is better cooked a day or two ahead. In Rumania it is soured by fermented wheat bran, unripened green grapes, green plums, sorrel leaves, and sauerkraut juice. Lemons, which may also be used, are a luxury there, but in this country sauerkraut juice and lemons are easier to come by than the other souring agents, so I have used them here.

BROTH

veal shank bones
pork bones from pork chops (see below under Meatballs)
2 large carrots, cut in half lengthwise
1 stalk celery with leaves, chopped
1 tomato, quartered
⅓ cup parsley sprigs
salt, pepper
1 quart sauerkraut juice or 1 cup lemon juice

Put the veal shank and pork bones into a large pot with 3 quarts of water. Bring to a boil; add the carrots, celery, tomato, parsley, salt, and pepper. Cover and simmer until the vegetables are tender. Pour in the sauerkraut juice and bring to a boil again. Cover and let stand off the heat while you prepare the meatballs.

MEATBALLS

½ lb. veal
½ lb. pork (cut from ¾ lb. of pork chops)
1 egg
salt, pepper
1 tablespoon finely chopped parsley
1 small onion, finely chopped
¼ teaspoon thyme
2 tablespoons raw rice
½ cup all-purpose flour

Grind the veal and pork with a fine blade. Mix the meat with the whole egg, salt, pepper, parsley, onion, thyme, and rice (which has been rinsed in cold water). Mix thoroughly with your hands and form into small balls the size of walnuts. Roll the meatballs in flour and let stand on a chopping board.

ASSEMBLY

2 tablespoons raw rice
1 stalk celery, chopped
1 lb. leeks, cut into 1-inch pieces
1 knob fennel, cut into pieces, with part of the green top minced
½ teaspoon thyme
⅓ cup chopped parsley
2 to 3 tarragon sprigs
1 piece of hot red pepper pod
1 cup sour cream, plus some for the topping
2 egg yolks, slightly beaten
1 tablespoon flour
1 tablespoon chopped fresh dill or tarragon,
or ½ teaspoon dried dill weed
chopped red or green hot peppers

Strain the broth into a clean pot and taste it. It should be rather sour, but it can be made less so by diluting with water, or more so by adding a bit more sauerkraut juice. Bring the broth to a boil and add two more tablespoons of rice rinsed in cold water. When the boiling starts, drop in the meatballs and the chopped celery, leeks, fennel, thyme, parsley, tarragon, and the hot pepper. Mix 1 cup sour cream in a bowl with the egg yolks and flour. Add a little cold water until you have a thin paste. Pour this into the ciorba, stirring constantly.

Let the soup boil slowly for 20 minutes with the pot covered to keep in the wonderful aroma. If possible, cool and allow to ripen in the refrigerator for 1 to 2 days, or freeze. Reheat and serve in large soup bowl, with a tablespoon of sour cream in each bowl. Sprinkle with dill or tarragon. On the side serve chopped red or green hot peppers.

Ciorba improves greatly with time, as the flavor continues to penetrate the ingredients. It must be kept tightly covered in the refrigerator, or it can be frozen in pint plastic containers. As Alice B. Toklas has said, "Who knows how many this will serve; it all depends how much you like it." But it should serve 6 to 8 generously.

Serve with pideh*; chocolate mousse*.

❧ NEW ENGLAND CLAM CHOWDER

Once upon a time I had New England clam chowder at its best, but it is seldom that the ingredients are all together at one time in their perfect state. Not only were the clams quiveringly fresh from the sea, but it was a perfect summer night on the Connecticut shore, the conversation was good, and the hostess was a superb and imaginative cook. Somehow there was a bit of leftover lobster in the house, and the butter in which lobsters had been dipped had been saved. The cut-up lobster and lobster-flavored butter were added to the chowder. Obviously, one can't always count on having leftover lobster and lobster butter, but happily I can say that it is difficult to make a bad clam chowder.

2 dozen clams or 3 10½-oz. cans minced clams
½ lb. diced lean salt pork
2 onions, diced
3 large potatoes, peeled and diced
2 cups milk
2 cups light cream
2 tablespoons butter
salt, pepper
Pilot or common crackers

Steam the clams until they open; drain and strain the clam juice and save. If you use canned minced clams, drain them well and save the juice. Add enough water to the juice to make 4 cups. Fry the salt pork in a deep saucepan until it browns; add the onions and cook slowly until they turn golden. Add the potatoes and clam juice. Bring to a boil, then turn down the heat and simmer until the potatoes are tender. Stir in the milk, cream, and the chopped clams and heat through. Do not boil. Take off the heat, add the butter, salt, and pepper, and stir again until the butter melts. Break the crackers into each soup bowl and pour on the chowder. Serve immediately. Serves 6 to 8.

Serve with salade Niçoise*; strawberry and raspberry granita*.

ᴥ§ OKROSHKA

Okroshka, one of the few substantial cold soups, is of Russian origin, although it is found throughout Eastern Europe. Traditionally, it is made with kvass, a fermented drink made from black bread. Kvass can be found in New York City, but most Americans are not fond of it (neither are some Russians). Instead, I use buttermilk, lemon juice, and vinegar.

⅓ cup chopped scallions, using some of the tops
1 teaspoon chopped fresh tarragon
3 tablespoons chopped fresh dill
or 1½ teaspoons dried dill weed
1 teaspoon salt
1 teaspoon sugar
freshly ground black pepper
1 tablespoon prepared mustard
1 tablespoon lemon juice
1 tablespoon vinegar
2 cups diced cooked meat (roast beef, chicken, or veal)
1 quart buttermilk, or 1 pint sour cream, thinned with
1 cup broth and 1 cup white wine
2 cups diced cucumbers
½ dill pickle, chopped
ice cubes
2 hard-cooked eggs, sliced
2 tablespoons finely chopped parsley

Put the scallions, tarragon, dill, salt, sugar, black pepper, mustard, lemon juice, and vinegar in a bowl and stir with a wooden spoon. Add the cooked meat, the buttermilk or diluted sour cream, diced cucumbers, and dill pickle. Stir well and chill.

Put an ice cube in each of 4 large, shallow bowls and pour in the soup mixture, making certain that each bowl has some of everything. Float a few slices of egg in the bowls, and sprinkle with parsley. Serves 4.

Serve with cold baked tomatoes stuffed with spinach; orange-peel ice*.

◄§ COLD SENEGALESE OR SINGHALESE SOUP

From time to time I forget how much I care about this soup, served cold on a hot day. It always seemed to me that it was a genteel descendant of a mulligatawny soup, and the name sounds like that of an Anglo-Indian dish—but Senegal is a West African country formerly belonging to France. Dione Lucas, however, called it Singhalese, which seems more likely, as if it originated in Ceylon, where the Singhalese people live. But I don't know and can find nothing specific about the origin of the recipe.

4 tablespoons butter
½ cup chopped onions
¼ cup chopped celery
1 tablespoon curry powder
2 tablespoons flour
4 cups chicken broth
1 cup diced cooked chicken (see poached chicken*)
⅔ cup peeled and chopped apple
1 pint light cream
½ apple, sliced and seeded but not peeled

Melt the butter in a deep kettle and cook the onion and celery for 2 or 3 minutes. Sprinkle with the curry powder and stir it in well. When the onions and the celery are soft but not browned, stir in the flour. Add the chicken broth, the diced cooked chicken, and chopped apple. Cook until the apple and the chicken are mushy and the whole soup is very fragrant. Blend in two batches in the blender and pour into a bowl. Add the cream and chill. To serve, ladle into small pretty bowls or soup mugs and top with thin slices of fresh apple. Serves 6.

Serve with lamb chops; raw mushroom salad* with watercress; Russian pistachio ice cream*.

⋙ WINTER-MELON SOUP

This is a dramatic dish for a party, especially when it is cooked and served in the melon. However, some Chinese culinary experts dispense with such nonsense. They cut the melon into pieces and cook it in a more straightforward fashion with the other ingredients, like a stew. It is much quicker that way, and the blend of flavors is just as interesting. The soup may be made with any simple or complex combination of traditional Chinese ingredients—shrimp, water chestnuts, scallions, green peas, lean ham, and so on. A large honeydew melon can be used in place of the winter melon if that is not available.

2 raw chicken breasts, boned, skinned, and cut in julienne strips
2 raw thin pork chops, boned, trimmed, and cut in julienne strips
2 thin slices fresh ginger
3 tablespoons dried mushrooms, soaked in warm water
½ cup bamboo shoots, diced, or 2 bunches watercress, chopped
1 small piece cooked Virginia ham, shredded,
or 2 pieces Canadian bacon, shredded
1 winter melon (5 to 6 lbs.)
salt, pepper

Put the chicken, pork, ginger, mushrooms, and bamboo shoots (but not the watercress) into a pot with as much water as one half the melon will hold. Simmer gently for 40 minutes, then add the ham. Meanwhile cut off the top of the melon and remove the seeds. Pour the mixture into the melon. (Add the watercress now if you are using that instead of the bamboo shoots.) Cover with the melon top. Stand the melon upright in a pot just a little larger. Pour water around it about 2 or 3 inches deep. Add salt and pepper. Steam for 1½ hours or until the melon is tender. Serve the melon on your best round platter, and ladle the soup into bowls at the table. With a spoon, scoop out some of the melon from the sides for each serving. After 2 or 3 inches have been scooped out, trim the skull of the melon neatly with a knife, for esthetic reasons. Serves 4 to 6.

Serve with roast turkey; barley and mushroom casserole; hot rolls; chocolate mousse*.

ᥰᥩ BRUNSWICK STEW

Brunswick stew originally used rabbit or squirrel meat instead of chicken; but chicken is now commonly used along with tomatoes, corn, lima beans, onions, and sometimes okra. In Virginia the stew is often cooked so that the vegetables are still distinguishable, but farther south the cooking time is much longer and the vegetables are likely to be cooked almost to a purée. This is the Virginia version.

2 chickens (about 2½ lbs. each), cut up
1 tablespoon salt
2 cups chopped onions
1 large can whole tomatoes, drained
1 lb. fresh shelled lima beans or 2 10-oz. packages frozen
1 box fresh okra or 1 10-oz. package frozen
2 cups whole kernel corn, fresh, frozen, or canned
½ teaspoon Tabasco sauce

Put the chicken in a large pot of water with the salt and cook slowly until tender, 45 minutes to 1 hour. Drain off the liquid, reserving the broth. Remove the meat from the bones and cut it into pieces. Put them into a pot with 2 cups of the broth and all the vegetables except the corn. Cook slowly until the limas are tender; add the corn and the Tabasco sauce for the last 15 minutes. Serves 4 to 6.

Serve with hush puppies; leaf lettuce with hot bacon dressing; pineapple sherbet with fresh strawberries.

ᥰᥩ CARBONNADE

A classic Belgian beef stew cooked with beer, which gives it a distinctive flavor.

flour
salt, freshly ground pepper

2 lbs. boneless beef, either rump or chuck,
cut into 2-inch cubes
6 medium onions, sliced
1 clove garlic, minced
3 tablespoons bacon fat
1 12-oz. bottle or can beer
1 tablespoon chopped parsley
1 bay leaf
¼ teaspoon thyme

Put the flour, salt, and pepper on a platter or in a paper bag and dust the pieces of meat thoroughly. In a large skillet cook the onion slices and garlic in the bacon fat until translucent and wilted but not brown. Remove the onion and garlic from the skillet with a slotted spoon. Add the meat and brown on all sides, adding more bacon fat if necessary. Add the cooked onion to the meat along with the beer, parsley, bay leaf, and thyme. Cover and cook over low heat until the meat is tender, about 1¼ hours. Serves 6 to 8.

Serve with boiled potatoes; hot rolls; sliced tomatoes and vinaigrette dressing and chopped fresh basil; macaroons*.

☙ GHIVECII

This is perhaps the most spectacular and beautiful way of cooking vegetables and tastes as good and as different as it looks. The number of vegetables you use varies with availability. A Rumanian hostess will pride herself on the number of different vegetables she has used and will tell you so that you will know just how special an occasion it is. A really impressive ghivech may have from twelve to eighteen different vegetables, but the traditional ones include: one of the cabbages (cauliflower, broccoli, Brussels sprouts, or red or green cabbage), tomatoes, potatoes, carrots, onions, and two or three green vegetables such as peas, green beans, and whatever others you can lay your hands on. The only vegetables never used are spinach, other cooked greens, and beets. This is not as extravagant a dish as it sounds, because just a handful of each vegetable is used. In some versions meat, preferably lamb or pork chops, is added at the last, but I like the vegetables by themselves. In order to cook and serve this, you should have a large, shallow casserole, either earthenware or the enameled ironware that is both colorful and practical.

1 head cauliflower or 1 bunch broccoli,
surplus leaves trimmed and stalks cut off
3 large potatoes, peeled and diced
4 carrots, scraped, sliced thin
1 eggplant, cut into large cubes with the peel left on
4 large tomatoes, quartered and seeds removed,
or 1 large can Italian plum tomatoes, drained
1 yellow squash, sliced thin but not peeled
4 or 5 medium-sized onions
1 cup fresh green peas
1 cup green beans, slivered or cut in pieces
1 green or red pepper, seeds removed, sliced thin
4 stalks celery, cut fine
2 cups soup stock
⅔ cup olive oil
4 or 5 cloves garlic, peeled (Rumanian version has much more)
1 tablespoon freshly chopped dill or mixed herbs
lots of salt, little pepper

Boil the cauliflower, potatoes, and carrots in salted water for about 15 minutes. Drain. Mix all the vegetables together, both raw and cooked, in the casserole. Heat the soup stock with the olive oil and the garlic cloves and pour it into the casserole. Sprinkle the top with the seasonings. In some parts of Rumania a bunch of white seedless grapes, pulled from the stem, are strewn around the top. This gives a delicate, acid touch that is very pleasing. Bake in a 350° oven for 1 to 1½ hours or until all vegetables are fork-tender. Because this dish was usually baked in the village oven and then brought home, it is customary to serve it lukewarm, and in fact the flavors are better when it is not served hot from the oven. I like to finish the cooking about an hour before dinner and let it cool slightly on the top of the stove.   Serves 6 to 8 generously.

Serve with roast lamb basted with tarragon vinegar; cheese and fresh pears; coffee.

❧ LAMB STEW WITH DILL

The fresh, clean flavor of dill enhances and "lifts" many dishes— meat, fish, soups, and salads alike.

2 lbs. lamb shoulder or breast, cut in pieces
8 small white onions, peeled and scored on end
3 large turnips, peeled and diced
1 teaspoon Kitchen Bouquet
1 tablespoon salt
4 peppercorns
1 bay leaf
2 sprigs fresh dill, slightly crushed,
or ½ teaspoon dried dill

DILL SAUCE

2 tablespoons butter
2 tablespoons flour
2 cups broth drained from stew
2 tablespoons chopped fresh dill
or 1 teaspoon dried dill weed
1 tablespoon vinegar
1 tablespoon sugar
salt, pepper
1 egg yolk, slightly beaten

Cover the meat, onions, and turnips with 2 cups (or more) boiling water in a Dutch oven.   Bring to a second boil and skim.   Add the seasonings.   Cover and cook in a 325° oven about 1 hour or until the meat and vegetables are tender. To make the sauce, melt the butter, add the flour, and stir over low heat until well blended. Add the broth slowly, stirring, until the sauce is smooth and thick. Add dill, vinegar, sugar, salt, and pepper to taste. Simmer 3 or 4 minutes. Remove from fire and stir in the egg yolk. Stir into the casserole. Do not cook further after adding the egg yolk. Serves 4.

Serve with sliced oranges and watercress with sour-cream dressing (½ cup sour cream with 1 teaspoon lemon juice); Swedish flat bread; coffee granita*.

⋅⋚ LAMB AND OKRA STEW

One of the few stews I like cooked with tomatoes. It is very color-ful, fresh looking, and hearty.

1 lb. fresh tender okra or 1 10-oz. package frozen okra
salt, pepper
1 lb. small white onions or 3 or 4 large yellow onions,
peeled and quartered
1½ lbs. boned lamb, cut up as for stew
2 tablespoons olive oil
1 lb. fresh tomatoes, peeled, seeded, and quartered, or 1 small can
1 lemon, cut in thin slices and seeded but not peeled

Wash the okra, put it in a bowl, and sprinkle with salt and pepper. Let it stand for half an hour. Brown the onions and the lamb in the oil in a Dutch oven or a deep, heavy skillet. Add 3 cups of water, cover, and simmer for 1 hour. Add the okra, tomatoes, and lemon and cook over low heat until okra is tender but not mushy. Serves 4.

Serve with pideh*; orange and black-olive salad*.

❧ LAMB SHANKS WITH DRIED FRUIT

One of my long-time favorites, and nicely economical, too.

4 lamb shanks
salt, pepper
flour
2 tablespoons butter
2 large cloves garlic, minced
1 10–12 oz. package mixed dried fruits
½ cup sugar
1 teaspoon cinnamon
½ teaspoon allspice
½ teaspoon ground cloves
¼ cup tarragon vinegar

Dust the lamb shanks with salt, pepper, and flour. Brown the meat with the garlic in the butter. Put in a large casserole with the dried fruits, sugar, seasonings, vinegar, and 3½ cups water. Cover tightly and bake in 350° oven for about 1½ to 2 hours or until the lamb shanks are tender. If time is short, use a pressure cooker at 15 pounds pressure for 45 to 55 minutes, depending upon the size of the shanks. Reduce the pressure gradually. Serves 4 to 6.

Serve with nut and currant pilaf (rice cooked in chicken broth with currants and sprinkled with slivered almonds); watercress; brownie pudding.

❧ MEATBALLS WITH DRIED-FRUIT SOUP

All the ingredients in this soup are things that might be found in any kitchen, but the combination of flavors, seasonings, and colors is unusual and very beguiling. The soup can be served either hot or cold and can be kept in the freezer. It is especially good served just partly thawed on a very hot day.

½ lb. chopped beef
1 small onion, grated
¼ teaspoon cinnamon
¼ teaspoon pepper
½ teaspoon salt
½ cup rice
1 small onion, chopped fine
2 tablespoons butter
1 cup dried prunes
1 cup dried apricots
¼ cup chopped walnuts
1 cup chopped parsley
¼ cup canned chickpeas, drained
½ cup vinegar
⅓ cup sugar

SOUP SPICE

1 tablespoon dried mint
¼ teaspoon cinnamon
¼ teaspoon pepper

Put the meat in a bowl, add the grated onion, cinnamon, pepper, and salt. Mix well and roll into small meatballs the size of walnuts. Bring 8 cups of salted water to a boil in a 3-quart pot. Add the rice and cook for 15 minutes. Meanwhile sauté the chopped onion in the butter and put aside. Add the prunes to the rice pot and cook for 15 minutes more. Add meatballs, apricots, walnuts, parsley, chickpeas, and sautéed onions. Cook for about 20 minutes over medium heat. Add the vinegar and sugar and cook for 15 minutes more. Rub the dried mint in the palm of your hands to make it powdery and to release the aroma. Add the cinnamon and pepper to the mint. Sprinkle this over the soup just before removing it from the fire. Check the other seasonings and add more salt and pepper if necessary. Serves 4 or 5.

Serve with cheese and smoked-oyster soufflé*; hot biscuits; coffee granita*; macaroons*.

~§ OXTAIL STEW

There are so many lovely odds and ends of meat that we tend to ignore. Take the oxtail, for instance, which makes one of the best of all stews. It is bought disjointed, either by the tail or by the pound, depending upon the region in which you live and the butcher you patronize. The stew is more robust when made with a head of cabbage, more delicate and traditionally European with celery root, or celeriac, a delicate root relative of our stalk celery. Fresh diced celery stalks may be used, but the texture is quite different.

> *1 or 2 oxtails, cut at the joint (about 3 lbs.)*
> *1 cup Burgundy*
> *4 onions, cut and quartered*
> *1 lemon, sliced thin, with seeds removed*
> *1 bay leaf, crumbled*
> *8 whole peppercorns*
> *1 teaspoon anchovy paste*
> *4 slices bacon, diced*
> *flour for dusting*
> *2 fat cloves garlic, cut in half*
> *3 cups beef broth*
> *4 carrots, peeled and quartered*
> *2 cups diced, peeled celery root or 1 cup diced celery stalks*
> *2 leeks, well washed and quartered and cut in 2-inch pieces*
> *½ cup dried mushrooms*
> *large bunch parsley, chopped*

Marinate the oxtails, preferably overnight but at least for several hours, in a mixture of the wine, onions, lemon, bay leaf, peppercorns, and anchovy paste. Sauté the bacon slowly in a skillet and drain the pieces on a paper towel. Remove the pieces of oxtail from the marinade and dust them with flour. Sauté the pieces of oxtail with the garlic in the bacon fat and transfer them (minus garlic) to a Dutch oven or a deep enamelware casserole. Pour in the marinade and broth, cover the pot, and bake for 2 hours in a 350° oven. Add the vegetables and bake for an hour more. Before serving, crumble the bacon on top. Serves 4.

Serve with cold boiled artichokes with heavily salted olive oil for dipping; Italian bread.

A Felicity of Sweets

Among my many clippings saved over the years is one from the late Julian Street's *Table Topics*, a delightful house organ that he edited for Bellows & Co., purveyors of wines and spirits. "Legend has it that the aunt of Brillat-Savarin shared his love of good food. She died at the age of 97 as she was finishing a rich dinner in her bed. 'I feel the end approaching,' she breathed. 'Quick bring me my dessert, coffee and liqueur.'" Apocryphal or not, this story should appeal to anyone who might wish to reach the end in style.

In the meantime, while we yet live, here are a few choice desserts not at all troublesome to make and good to keep in mind for guests, or for other times of ceremonious indulgence. Even those who do not much feel the need for desserts, and I am one of these, have an occasional yearning for such goodies as a very rich chocolate mousse, grapefruit Alaska, fresh strawberries with a zabaglione sauce, glazed oranges, crème brûlée, or perhaps a chocolate broyage with a velvety and voluptuous filling of more chocolate.

The dessert, that frivolous, subtly hedonistic finish to a meal, should complement and contrast with the preceding dishes in color, flavor, and texture. A heavy main dish might be followed by a light dessert such as glazed oranges, coffee granita, or a fresh lemon mousse, while the partaker of a light entrée could certainly deal with a more ample dessert, such as a rich mousse.

Select a serving dish or plate in a shape or texture that enhances the appearance of the dessert. It needn't be expensive; a ring mold of watermelon sherbet with blueberries or black Bing cherries in the center looks beautiful in clear glass or in dark ironware. A deep chocolate brown dessert, however, would be nicely set off by a silver bowl or a pretty handmade piece of pottery.

◄§ GLAZED ORANGES

This fresh, sophisticated, decorative way of serving fresh oranges is known in many Mediterranean countries by a surprising variety of names. I much prefer it to ambrosia, the Southern way of serving fresh sliced oranges with coconut.

4 fresh seedless oranges
1 cup sugar
pinch of cream of tartar
¼ cup curaçao or other orange-flavored liqueur

Peel the oranges with a swivel-blade vegetable peeler very thinly, being careful not to take any of the white pith. Cut the peel into very fine julienne strips. Put the peel in water, bring to a boil, then drain. In a saucepan heat 1½ cups of water and dissolve the sugar in it. Add the cream of tartar and drained orange peel. Bring to a boil and simmer until thickened, for 5 or 6 minutes. Take off the fire and add the liqueur. Chill. Peel the oranges again with a sharp knife, removing all pith, and cut into slices about ¼ inch thick. Arrange in the serving dish and pour the syrup and peel over them. Serves 4.

Serve after lamb curry; rice; cucumber and fennel salad with oil-and-vinegar dressing; and with espresso.

◄§ STRAWBERRIES WITH ZABAGLIONE

This dish is a real life-enhancer with its hot sauce and cold fruits. The same sauce may be served alone, as the Italians often do, or with other soft fruits, say sliced fresh peaches. However, strawberries seem the most inspired and the most decorative. When served alone, zabaglione is traditionally made with Marsala.

8 egg yolks
8 teaspoons sugar
¾ cup dry white wine
¼ cup curaçao or any other good orange liqueur
pinch of powdered ginger
2 cups whole fresh strawberries, hulled

Beat the egg yolks and the sugar together until lemon colored. Stir in the wine liqueur, and ginger and pour into a heavy saucepan. Cook over low heat, stirring until thickened. It must not boil or it will curdle. Pour over the strawberries or pass it in a sauceboat at the table. Serves 4.

Serve after broiled chicken breasts; capellini*; Italian green bean salad*.

⇜ STRAWBERRY FRITTERS

I like fritters of various kinds in theory, but I actually seldom make them. I'm not sure why—they appeal to many people and are simple to do. Here is one recipe I do come back to again and again. The beer batter makes for an especially delicate fritter, and does not taste of beer. Vegetable oil is best for frying this type of fritter; it may be strained and stored in the refrigerator and used again for frying the same type of flavor. This means, of course, that you cannot expect to use oil in which you have fried fish for something as delicate as strawberries.

1½ cups light beer
1 cup flour
1 tablespoon salt
1 tablespoon sugar (omit for nonsweet fritters)
1 quart whole fresh strawberries
oil for frying (about 2 quarts)

Mix the beer and flour, salt, and sugar. Let it stand for at least 30 minutes. Wash, pat dry, and hull the strawberries. Heat the fat to 375°. Dip the strawberries, a few at a time, in the batter and lower in a frying basket into the hot fat. When they get brown and turn over and float, they are done. Drain on the paper towels and keep them warm while you are doing the rest. Serves 6 to 8.

Serve after cheese and smoked-oyster soufflé*; Persian mäst*.

৺ৡ WIENER GOTTSPEISE
(FOOD OF THE GODS)

In this extravagantly named Viennese dessert, macaroons are for me the most important part, though the strawberries are the most noticeable. It is an exuberant cousin to the daintier tortoni.

1 egg yolk
2 tablespoons rum
5 tablespoons sugar
1 cup macaroon crumbs
1 cup heavy cream, whipped stiff
1 pint strawberries

Beat the egg yolk with the rum and 2 tablespoons of the sugar and stir in the macaroon crumbs. Fold in the stiffly beaten cream. Turn into a greased 2½-to-3-cup mold. Keep in the freezer until firm. Wash, hull, and dry the strawberries and sweeten them with 3 tablespoons (or more) of sugar. To serve, unmold on a glass or silver plate and surround with the sugared strawberries. Serve firm. Serves 6 to 8.

Serve after mutton ham (see recipe for flageolets à la crème) or the more familiar kind; black beans and rice; cucumber and fennel salad.

CRÈME BRÛLÉE (BURNT CREAM)

In both French and English the name of the dish is imprecise, for what is browned or burnt is the sugar topping. It is a simple classic dish of rich creamy unsweetened custard with a dark crust of sugar.

> *2 cups heavy cream*
> *1 inch of vanilla bean*
> *4 egg yolks, well beaten*
> *brown sugar or praline powder**

Bring the cream and vanilla bean slowly to the boiling point. Boil for 1 minute, no more. Pour into the well-beaten egg yolks, stirring constantly with a whisk. (An alternative method is to blend the egg yolks and pour the hot cream into the container of the electric blender while it is still running at a slow speed.) When mixed, pour into the top of a double boiler over simmering water or into a heavy enamel saucepan and cook for about 5 minutes, or until the custard coats a wooden spoon. Pour the custard into a shallow buttered baking dish or buttered individual custard cups and chill until it becomes firm but still a little trembly looking. (This may be done the day before if you like.) About an hour or two before dinner, not much longer, cover the entire surface of the custard with a ¾-inch layer of sugar or praline powder. Place under a preheated broiler, leaving the door open until the sugar has melted and formed a crust. While this is happening, you must be sharply observant, since the custard is all too likely to burn. Chill again during dinner. Serves 4.

Serve after carbonnade* with spaetzle*; raw mushroom salad* with watercress; French or Italian bread.

FROZEN ALEXANDERS

I could never understand why genteel ladies used to like such a sweet rich drink as this, and I don't think many people do nowadays.

The late Poppy Cannon thought of serving Alexanders for dessert, which is where they really belong, somewhat in the manner of cold Irish coffee.

> *1 cup crème de cacao*
> *1 cup brandy or gin*
> *1 cup heavy whipping cream*
> *4 cups finely chopped ice*

Mix the ingredients together and put half in a chilled blender container and whirl until smooth. Repeat with the other half and serve in chilled dishes. Serves 8 voluptuously.

Serve after Siamese curry*; Persian mäst*.

✑ CHOCOLATE MOUSSE

This blender version was first worked out by Alice B. Toklas in an article in *House Beautiful,* and it later became part of Ms. Toklas's book *Aromas and Flavors.* She tops the mousse with a Cointreau-flavored whipped cream, but I think the mousse rich enough in it-self with the cream in it, so I have added the Cointreau directly. This is a decorative and dramatic dessert when served in pots de crème, those little pottery cups that aren't too difficult to come by these days.

> *½ lb. melted Swiss or French sweet chocolate,*
> *or half and half sweet and bitter chocolate*
> *1 cup heavy cream*
> *1 cup confectioners' sugar*
> *8 eggs, separated*
> *pinch of salt*
> *jigger of Cointreau or cognac*

Melt the chocolate *over* hot water, not in it, and pour it into the glass container of the blender with the cream, sugar, egg yolks, salt, and liqueur. Blend until it is all one color, for 2 or 3 minutes. Add the egg whites and blend 2 or 3 minutes more. Chill in pots de crème or a pretty glass bowl. Serves 4.

Serve after parsleyed ham*; gnocchi verdi*; raw mushroom salad*.

ᴥᶴ KEY LIME PIE

The traditional Key lime pie made with canned condensed milk evolved in Florida when refrigeration was haphazard and milk was in uncertain supply and of unreliable quality. The filling is not cooked but thickened by the chemical action of the lime juice. In this recipe it is used with an untraditional nut crust and then, again untraditionally, with thin slices of lime on the top.

1 14-oz. can sweetened condensed milk
4 egg yolks
½ cup lime juice
2–3 drops of green food coloring (optional)
1 nut pie crust (8-inch)*
2 limes, sliced very thin

Mix the condensed milk, egg yolks, lime juice, and coloring thoroughly. The juice will cook the eggs. Pour into the pie shell and chill. When slightly firm, arrange the very thin lime slices in a slightly overlapping circle over the top. Chill until you are ready to serve. Serves 4 generously.

Serve after parsleyed chicken*; mushroom risotto*, Bibb lettuce with cream dressing*.

✑ OAK LEAVES

These are to me the most beautiful and elegant of all small cakes, with the exquisite flavor of almond paste subtly pointed up by the chocolate. Serve them at a formal tea or for dessert, along with espresso, or as an accompaniment to another sweet. One can buy metal leaf stencils in many cookware shops, but it is simple enough to draw around an oak leaf on a piece of cardboard and cut out the design yourself. Place the stencil on the thin rolled dough and cut around it with a blunt knife for the traditional design.

1 8-oz. can almond paste
¾ cup sifted flour
½ cup sugar
2 tablespoons melted butter
2 lightly beaten egg whites
1 6-oz. package semi-sweet chocolate morsels
1 tablespoon vegetable oil

Crumble the almond paste with your fingers and add the flour, sugar, and melted butter. Mix well and stir in the egg whites. The batter or dough should be very soft, but since the size of egg whites is variable and moisture in the air will affect the flour, you may need to try this recipe several times until you learn how to judge the consistency best. If the batter seems too stiff, add another egg white. Butter a cookie sheet and dust it with flour. Spread the dough very thinly over the sheet and, using the stencil, cut out your oak leaves. Reroll the excess dough and make new leaves. Bake in a preheated 350° oven for 10 to 12 minutes, or until pale yellow. Watch carefully because they burn easily. Transfer them gently to a counter covered with wax paper.

After the cookies have cooled, turn them over carefully. Melt the chocolate with the vegetable oil over hot water. Spread the bottoms of the leaves smoothly and thinly with the chocolate. Take a toothpick and mark the veins lightly on each leaf. This will make about 18 leaves about 3 inches long.

If you are having trouble getting the right consistency, you can practice with the macaroon mix that comes in a tube at some supermarkets. Spread it thinly, bake, and cover with chocolate. It is not exactly the same, because it has no flour, but the flavor is almost the same and it is much easier to work with. The most important thing to achieve is the almost cardboard thinness. One tube makes about the same number as this recipe. Makes 18 cookies.

Serve after seafood casserole*; rice; Bibb lettuce with vinaigrette dressing; and with espresso.

ᵔᵏ CHOCOLATE TRUFFLES

This is the only candy I ever make, having escaped any contact with fudge-making parties in my youth. These are easy to do, expensive to buy, and taste, as a friend of mine put it, "like pure gold." They also make very welcome gifts—to take, not send, for they are much too perishable for the mails.

½ lb. semi-sweet chocolate
(though sweet Swiss or French chocolate is best)
⅓ cup milk
⅓ cup unsalted butter (⅔ stick)
2 large egg yolks
cocoa (unsweetened, not instant)

Melt the chocolate with the milk over hot water, stirring until smooth. Add the butter and stir until blended. Add the egg yolks, mix with the chocolate, and chill until firm (about 2 hours). Take a small melon scoop and make little balls about the diameter of a nickel. Roll them in cocoa and chill or freeze. These keep their shape better when packaged in layers without mashing. Candy boxes with the small paper dishes used by commercial bakeries are fine for these. Ask a candy store where to buy them wholesale. This will make approximately 4 to 6 dozen. Store in the freezer or refrigerator.

Index

231